Mary Destiny

"Normally, one would think a story about one family's experiences, as their father battles cancer, would be depressing. Instead, *Through a Daughter's Eyes* is an uplifting personal exploration of the powerful bonds of family. Offering flashbacks viewed through the eyes of a perceptive teenage daughter, Mary DeJong shares her story using loving memories of seemingly mundane day-to-day family living, interspersed with update letters sent to friends and family. Love, positivity, and faith are the themes. This is a must-read for anyone who has experienced or wishes to truly understand the power of hope, love, and a faith that overcomes the trials of cancer's roller coaster ride."

—**GAIL COWDIN**, author of *Deception and Redemption: A Quay Thompson Novel*

"*Through a Daughter's Eyes* is a heartbreaking, beautiful story about a family's journey as they navigate life with their husband and father who is battling cancer. Mary shows how an amazing support system and strong faith guides them as they face some of their toughest challenges and come out stronger in the end."

—**ASHLEY CHISHOLM**, Instagram Literary Personality @minnesota_mailer

"An exquisitely written book that brings to life the core meaning of the words 'love,' 'compassion,' and 'integrity' that so many people in the world are searching for in their own lives. It should be read everywhere by everyone. I have spent my life doing complex and sometimes incompletely understood procedures on patients at the University of Minnesota. Many patients get to us after other care-givers feel that they have nothing more to offer. Sometimes there is nothing we can do. Sometimes we can offer a slight increase in lifespan or a decrease in pain or disability. It is only infrequently that we are we able to offer a cure or a definitive solution. Each patient responds to this dilemma differently so we try never to exceed a patient's wishes. Tom was a very special patient, one of very few, who had the strength of character to accept and appreciate our limitations, and welcome whatever we could do to help. He was as exceptional as the book portrays him, and his family was even stronger and more loving than they give themselves credit for. This beautifully written love story brought back powerful memories that frequently brought me to tears. Tom was one of those people who inspired others around him to be greater, bolder, more caring, and more loving than they might have been. I am honored and humbled to have played a small role in his life. This is the story of a man who was a great man because of how he enriched the lives of those who surrounded him. Although he lost his body, his spirit never faltered. The book is an exquisite jewel of affection and emotional truth. If you read it slowly and with your heart open, this book will give you the recipe for how that magic happens."

> —**David Hunter, MD**, Retired Professor of Interventional Radiology, University of Minnesota

"Through a Daughter's Eyes is heartfelt, tear-jerking, and wonderful. I, too, lost my dad to this terrible disease. Afterward, I wanted the Roger Maris Cancer Center to be set up for other families, like Mary's, in their battle with this far too common disease."

> —**Roger Maris, Jr.**, son of baseball legend Roger Maris

"The descriptions of family and the events the DeJong family went through create an emotional story that is relatable since so many others have gone through similar hardships with their families. It's so tough to lose a loved one, and *Through a Daughter's Eyes* definitely touched on the emptiness of what it feels like when a family's dad is gone."

—**Bart Maris**, Roger Maris family lawyer

"Through a Daughter's Eyes taught me, an oncologist, the reality for a child or teenager to live through the sad reality of cancer affecting a parent. We can only live in the present, hoping that the progress in medicine will benefit our children and grandchildren. Mary's father taught us a lot about the treatments that failed to cure his cancer. The lessons learned do benefit future patients. I am very grateful that she wrote this book."

—**Louis Geeraerts, MD**

Through a Daughter's Eyes

by Mary DeJong

ISBN 978-1-63393-906-6

Published by

 köehlerbooks ™

210 60th Street
Virginia Beach, VA 23451
800–435–4811
www.koehlerbooks.com

THROUGH
A
Daughter's
EYES

MARY DEJONG

VIRGINIA BEACH
CAPE CHARLES

To my mom and sisters.
We've come so far.

CHAPTER 1

"THAT'S WHAT, H-O-R-S TO NOTHING?"

"Shut up, Mary," Emma said to me, clearly defeated. "I don't even know why I play this with you."

Smiling to myself, I decided to push her a little further. "Here, Emma. Try this one."

I took the ball ten feet away from the hoop to where the free throw line would be. Taking one power dribble, I made my way to the basket, extending my strides as far as they could go. The perfect layup.

"You know," she told me as she confidently made her way to the base of the hoop, "I don't have to do that. I only have to shoot from where you did. None of that fancy-shmancy stuff."

Emma was short, only about 5'4" to my 5'7". She held the ball in her hand as she put all of her weight on one leg, popped her hip, and threw her hair over her shoulder. She waited for my response.

"Yeah, right," I said. "You have to do exactly what I do. That's how you play the game."

"Nope. I have to shoot from where you do. *That's* how you play."

I just looked at her. Emma was fifteen and, therefore, a H-O-R-S-E expert. She had never played an official game of basketball in her life, but she was older than me, and so naturally, she knew everything.

"It's okay, I guess." I smiled at her. "It's not like you have a chance at winning this game anyway."

It was about seven o'clock in the evening and still hot as ever. Jake and Jamison had both been over earlier that afternoon, but they had gone home to eat dinner with their families. They'd most likely be back again later.

Jamison was a year younger than Emma. He was slim and didn't quite measure up to my giant status. He was always wearing a white t-shirt, athletic shorts, and a baseball cap. Always. He spent most of his time, when he wasn't at our house, running on various track and cross country teams. He rarely lost and always made fun of me for not sharing his natural speed, but he was one of the few people I knew who could beat me in any kind of running race.

Jake was the same age as me – thirteen. We'd always been close, ever since early elementary school. He was an athlete, but he was struggling in the height department. He, like Jamison, always wore athletic clothing. He had brown hair, a big smile, and his skin stayed a constant tan year-round. In the third grade, Jake drew a picture of him and me together during church that said "Jacob and Mary" across the top. When he and his family returned home that day, his dad approached him, picture in hand. When he asked what it was, Jake stormed towards him, grabbed the picture, tore it up, and threw it away, crying the entire time.

"Incoming," Emma warned me. "Stacy alert."

But it was too late. Stacy was already on our driveway, nearing us with every step.

Our neighbor across the street, Stacy, was one of those ladies who liked to talk. About herself. Nonstop. She had the outstanding ability to go on and on about her kids, her failed marriage, her job, her new hairstyles, and even her grocery lists, completely oblivious to our not-so-subtle, "Okay, well, it's really getting late," or, "Well, Mom said we needed to be in by seven."

"Hello, ladies." Her voice was slow and fairly low for a middle-aged woman. It had a drone to it that made it seem as if anything she talked about was not even worth her own time.

"Hi, Stacy," Emma replied with a slightly too forced smile. "What's up?"

"Oh, you know." Of course we did. "Hannah's getting into all kinds of trouble again."

Hannah was her twelve-year-old daughter who made it very clear that she did not want to live with her mother and stepfather, but with her biological father instead.

"Oh, that's too bad," Emma politely sympathized.

"Yeah, she snuck out again last night." Twelve and sneaking out of the house? Jeez.

"Yikes, that sounds awful."

"Yep. Anyway," she sighed, "how's Dad?" I felt a lump form in my throat.

"He's good. Mom's in with him now." Emma lied, hoping to shorten the conversation as much as possible.

The truth was, Dad wasn't *good*. Not even remotely okay. The cancer had spread to his brain, and he was forgetting who we were. Just hearing them talk about him made me force my attention elsewhere, not even considering how rude that may be. Not only did I leave the conversation, but I was endangering the two of them as they stood near the basket, and I began to run the Mikan drill, throwing the ball up in continuous layups. Jump, shoot, turn, catch. Jump, shoot, turn, catch.

Concentrate, I told myself. My record at camp was thirty-five in one minute. *Come on, don't listen to them talk. Just beat it.*

The door to the garage opened. *Twenty-eight, twenty-nine, thirty . . .* I could hear footsteps coming down the stairs inside the garage to the ground level. *Thirty-one, thirty-two, thirty-three . . .*

"Girls, you need to come inside." Nothing could break my concentration. *Thirty-four, thirty-five . . .*

"Emma. Mary. Come inside."

Stacy stopped talking. Nobody said anything, leaving a silence to hang over us. This time when I landed, I didn't jump back up to the hoop again. I held the ball and turned around to face Emma and Stacy. Emma was staring into the garage with big eyes. I followed her gaze. My mom stood in the garage, eyes red and puffy, her cheeks all wet.

"Mom," I began to say.

"Come inside," she said. Without hesitation, I dropped the ball to the ground and ran to follow her.

Emma and I were out playing in the living room with our Barbies on the day that my mom called us back into her bedroom. "Girls, I need to talk to you about something. Please come back to my room," she said. Emma hopped up from the floor, dropped her Barbie, and ran to the back bedroom where three-year-old Claire and my mom were already waiting. I decided it was best if I took my sweet time in the living room. What was the rush? They were all waiting for me to join them, and this would bother Emma. I'll take my time.

"Mary, please come back here," Mom called from the back room. From the living room, I could look down the hallway to see if she was looking. Her head was poking out of the doorway at me, but she was not giving me her usual threatening glare. Whenever I challenged my mom, she would develop a look that seemed to say, "Don't push me." This time, oddly enough, she didn't.

Wondering what was so important that she had to tell the three of us at the same time, I slowly stood up and wandered down the hallway towards where she stood. Emma and Claire were sitting on the edge of my parents' bed, their legs dangling off the blue-and-white plaid bedspread. Claire was wearing a hot pink tutu and ballet slippers with white tights covering her tiny legs. She always wore little dance uniforms whenever Mom would let her, and she liked to dance instead of walk wherever she went. At night, we could often find Claire upstairs in the living room with the ceiling light dimmed, music playing, passionately dancing by herself; she liked to call it "Moonlight Dancing."

Emma shot me an annoyed glare, so I ran over to her and jumped up onto the bed, plopping myself directly next to her, slightly too close for her comfort. She sighed and crossed her arms at me in response. "Finally," she muttered under her breath.

"Girls," my mom began. She still held that same expression on her face. She was serious, but concerned at the same time — almost sad, but also almost worried. It was a face I hadn't seen on her before.

I wasn't sure what to expect. My mind thought of everything I had done throughout the past two days. Was I in trouble for something? Did Emma tell on me for something I said or did? But if that was true, why did Emma and Claire have to be here, too?

"I'm about to tell you something very serious," she said slowly, "but that doesn't mean I want you to be scared." She paused, trying to find the right words. "You know that Dad and I have been going to the doctor's office lately. He always feels like he has to go to the bathroom when he acutally doesn't, and when he does, it hurts him." The three of us sat there quietly and listened to her talk.

"The doctor did some tests on his stomach, and he told us that Dad is sick. He has something called cancer. He has a tumor on his rectum, his bottom, that you can feel from outside of his body. Do you know what cancer is?" We didn't. "Cancer is when

something grows inside your body that fights the good cells in your body. It can be very dangerous, but the doctor told us that if Dad has to have cancer, this is a good kind to have. We caught it early, and it is easy to get rid of. That being said, we still wanted you to know what was going on."

"How will they get rid of it?" Emma asked her. I hadn't even considered that there was a way to get rid of sickness. I thought it was something he could get over after taking some sick days from work, like a head cold or something.

"Eventually, Dad will need to have surgery to remove his tumor, but they want to shrink it a little bit first. There are two different treatments the doctors want to try on him," she explained. "Radiation and chemotherapy. Radiation is small like a laser, where they point it directly at the tumor to kill it. Chemotherapy is a kind of poison that will kill all fast-growing cells in his body. Cancer grows very quickly, but so does hair. So he may lose his hair." She took a second to look at us. I was following everything she told us, and although Claire was still looking at her, her eyebrows were furrowed together, showing that Mom had lost Claire's understanding some time ago.

"He's going to be bald?" Claire asked, addressing the only part of what Mom had just said that she understood. My mom smiled at her, leaned forward to put her hand on her knee, and nodded to answer her question.

"We will bring you girls down to the hospital to see where he will do his treatments. It's not a scary place at all. After Dad goes through a couple of rounds of chemo and six weeks of radiation, he will have his surgery. They'll go inside his stomach and remove the tumor, along with part of his colon. That's the tube that your food goes through on its way out of your body."

"Wait, so where will the food go?" I asked her. "How will Dad go to the bathroom?"

"He will get something called a colostomy," she told me. She layered her hands on top of each other and placed them low on her stomach. "He will have something that looks like lips coming out of his stomach right here. He will have a small bag, or a colostomy pouch, over it because that's where his colon will end."

"So Dad will go to the bathroom out of his stomach?" Emma asked.

"Sort of, yes." She nodded.

CHAPTER 2

AUTOPILOT TOOK OVER MY BODY, and I subconsciously ran back to my parents' room. I stopped in the doorway and looked around; Beth, my mom's sister, was sitting in a recliner next to my dad's bed with tears running down her face, while Claire stood next to her, her face serious. My mom had gone to my dad's bedside with her back turned to us.

Grandma Fidler was walking towards me and as she cried, she was muttering something I couldn't quite make out. She dipped her fingers into a small container she was holding and touched them to my forehead. As the liquid dripped off my face, I looked at Emma who was standing beside me, and I shot her a confused expression.

"She's praying," she whispered. "The water's some Catholic thing."

I walked past my grandma to make my way to Dad's bed. He wasn't breathing. His eyes were motionless, fixed to a single spot high in the corner of the room. He held a constant expression on his face, which was a strange color, having a sort of yellow tint to it.

"Hold his hand," my mom said to me, and I realized she had been watching me. But I shook my head and looked down towards the floor under his hospice bed, backing up slowly, and felt the tears begin to fall.

"Mary?" I heard my mom call after me, but I wasn't looking up. I wasn't going to look at my Dad like that. I had so many memories of him, so many images of him laughing and smiling. I didn't want to ruin those with what I had just seen.

I headed straight to the phone in the kitchen.

"Hello?"

"Hi, Diane." It took everything in me to keep my voice stable. "Is Danielle there?"

"Mary? Is that you?"

I nodded. I knew she couldn't see me, but I wasn't sure I could handle answering without letting it all go. As if she could read my mind, I heard talking in the background.

"Hello?"

"Danielle . . . I . . . " I took a second to breathe. "He's gone. I think he's really gone."

"I'll be right over."

MAY 27, 2003

Since most of you have inquired about my health condition over the past couple of months, I want to let you know what the current status is.

Last week Becky and I went to the University of Minnesota to get additional opinions on how to treat my cancer. My oncologist here is offering chemotherapy as his option, but we felt there had to be more that could be done. Here is what we found out. On Wednesday, May 21, we met with a thoracic surgeon, Dr. Dahl. He was easy to talk to and explained everything very well. He did say that I have plenty of good lung to work with. He said there are about ten spots (six on one lung, four on the other) that he would investigate for removal. He is very confident that removal of the ten spots is an option, but only if we get the primary site (tumor in the pelvic area) under control. Until then, he would not recommend lung surgery. We expected his answer, so we were not totally disappointed when we walked out.

That afternoon, we met with the doctor who would be treating the tumor in the pelvic area. His name is Dr. Fisher, and we found out he is known throughout the world for his expertise (kind of comforting!). Without looking at previous pictures and only reading documentation of my history, he said his goal was to treat whatever part of the tumor he could to provide pain relief. His goal was not to remove it totally because of its complexity. It is located in the pelvic area around many nerves going to the leg and close to other internal parts that I don't really need to go into. The procedure is done using CT scans, and they call it a "CT Guided Radiological Obliteration" of the tumor. This would start on Thursday! Before we left, I had some blood taken for analysis. As this was happening, Becky saw the nurse give Dr. Fisher all of my previous x-rays and images from CT scans and PET scans. She told him this was complicated.

When the procedure started, they gave me some medication for pain relief and said that I would be awake, but would not remember too much of what happened. I do remember talking to the nurse and asking questions on how things were going. She would always say "fine" and smile. I wanted to know specifically what was happening, and I think she got tired of my questions. I also said that I could tell I had some pain medication but felt okay. She said my eyes indicated that I had medication. As Dr. Fisher progressed, I asked him how things were going. He did three biopsies (all indicated cancer). He did tell me everything went better than he had expected and that he was halfway done. He was looking forward to Friday to finish the other half. Before leaving, I had them show me the needles they were using. They couldn't understand why, but showed me anyway. Basically, they inserted one needle to be used like a conduit. The other needles would be inserted through this one. Each of the needles was four to five inches in length!

Friday came and things went well. When Dr. Fisher was finished, I asked him how things went. He was extremely pleased. He indicated that the tumor was about one and a half inches from top to bottom. He was able to treat it 100 percent from top to bottom and 75 percent from side to side. He said things were definitely under control and to start scheduling surgery for the lungs. He wanted me to come back in a month or so to finish killing the tumor in the pelvic area. To sum it up, instead of a prognosis of always having cancer and trying to live with it in remission, Dr. Fisher said they could cure me! He would keep treating the tumor in the pelvic area until it is 100 percent dead and gone. This summer will involve those further treatments with Dr. Fisher, two lung surgeries, and some chemo treatments. Sounds kind of busy, but the outcome sounds promising.

Needless to say, we had a happy household for Memorial Day weekend. We still have a long way to go, but there appears to be light at the end of the tunnel. Thanks for all your thoughts and prayers you have given us.

Tom

I tied my shoelaces up tight and looked at Mom in the living room and sighed. She was sitting on the couch doing a puzzle in one of her puzzle books. She looked up at me when she realized I was looking in her direction, and she smiled at my expression.

"You told him you wanted to go with him next time," she said to me.

"He goes so far," I said with a hint of complaining in my voice. "And it's so early."

"Well," she paused as she closed the puzzle book and put it in her lap, "you like to run. You can keep up with him. And he usually doesn't go in the mornings, but we are busy tonight, so this is when there is time. He's already outside waiting for you."

I looked outside through the window in the front door to see Dad stretching. He had his right foot propped up on one of the cement stairs leading to the front door. With his weight on his left leg, he leaned into his propped up foot to stretch the muscles of his leg in preparation for our workout. I walked up to the door to head outside, and before I could touch the knob, he looked up at me and smiled. He stood up from his stretch and waved, motioning for me to come outside and join him.

I was wearing a ragged gray sweatshirt with a few holes in the front. The material had grown thin, and the elastic did not constrict anymore with its age. The back of the sweatshirt had screen printed letters that read "Iroquois Track" and underneath was the number eleven. It was an obviously well-worn sweatshirt of Dad's from high school that he had found when going through some of his old boxes, and he let me keep it. It was in horrible shape, but because it was Dad's and it said "Track" on it, I liked to wear it on our runs.

"Morning, sunshine," he said to me sarcastically as I opened the door and stepped outside, almost blinded by the sunlight beaming against the side of the house. I made my way down the steps and then turned around to join in stretching with him. As I extended my arms and rested my hands on my lower shins, I felt him put a hand on my back and gently push me further forward, forcing me to actually stretch rather than pretend.

"Too early," I sleepily mumbled at him.

"You'll be fully awake by the time we reach the end of the block," he said. "And when we get home, you can go inside and bug your sisters for still being asleep."

We walked down to the end of the driveway together and planned our route. We always started the same way by taking a left and going straight until we hit a fork at the end of our street, and from there, each of our runs took us to different streets and neighborhoods.

As we began, my feet felt heavy, and it took me a while to find my stride. The morning air was cold. The grass, slightly frosted, had grown long and now covered the edges of the sidewalks, and the cement almost shimmered in the morning sunlight. It was late fall, so there wasn't snow on the ground yet, but still, taking deep breaths stung my lungs. I tried to breathe in through my nose and out through my mouth, but I needed more air than that, so I dealt with the cold.

Dad's strides were long and even. His breathing was steady; it was as if he could run forever without getting tired. He never seemed out of breath until he stopped running altogether. I ran alongside him with similar, but shorter, strides and wondered if I'd ever master the same breathing techniques he had probably figured out a long time ago.

He started to distance himself from me as he ran, moving towards the grass on the left side of the sidewalk. Continuing to run, he leaned over the grass, plugged his right nostril with his fingers, and blew his nose into the iced grass next to him.

"Yuck," I tried to yell at him between my heaving breaths. "That's disgusting."

"But necessary," he said without struggle. I noticed that none of this had interrupted his neat strides or his pace. "Sometimes you gotta do what you gotta do." He looked down towards me as he ran. "Try it."

"What? No."

"Do it. It's relieving," he said. "This cold makes your nose run. You'd be amazed at how much easier it is to breathe after."

Trying to keep my stride, I leaned over the grass to my right to mimic what I had just seen him do. I plugged my left nostril and blew hard onto the grass. Whatever came out of my nose, though, didn't quite make it to the ground. I felt stickiness and wetness low on my cheek, and I quickly bunched up the sleeve of my sweatshirt to wipe it off. Either he didn't notice or he pretended not to notice.

"See?" he asked. "Better, right?"

"Yeah, lots better." If he was pretending, I was going to play along.

"Want to head towards home to drop you off?" he asked me. "Or are you in for the long haul?" Sometimes, when Dad wanted to go on longer runs he would make our house a halfway point, and I would stay there as he passed. I liked to shoot hoops in the driveway while I waited for him to come back around the corner, and I would join him in his jump rope or ab exercises to finish our workouts.

"No," I said. "I'll stay with you today."

CHAPTER 3

EMMA WAS CRYING. I HAD cried a few times about my dad, but I had never seen her cry. Not even once. She was hugging my uncle Mike, Beth's husband, in the living room, and Mike just stood there holding her as she cried. My cousins, Tate and Mitchell, were sitting on the couch with Beth, and they seemed uncomfortable, as if they didn't know what they were supposed to do or what they were supposed to say. They couldn't tell if I needed them to help me the same way Mike was there for Emma, or if I needed them to leave me alone and be by myself.

The door from the garage opened and Danielle welcomed herself inside. That's how you know when someone is your best friend. They bike over to your house when you need them, and they don't bother to knock when they get there.

Danielle was my exact height and had thick blond hair that was always pulled tight into a ponytail in the back of her head.

I walked past her, making my way to the swing outside on the driveway. She turned around, and slowly she followed my lead. Together we sat in silence — she knew that's exactly what I needed.

"How'd it happen?" she finally asked me.

"He just stopped breathing. I didn't see it, though. I guess he took a few short breaths, and then he just stopped. That's what Mom said."

She nodded.

We heard the door open from inside the garage and the footsteps of someone walking down the three steps to the ground level.

"Hey, girls," Beth said. "Matt will be here any minute, so we're going to need you to come inside."

Matt Stith was the minister at our church, and he was coming to bless Dad's body and pray with everyone in the room.

As we walked back inside, I heard a car door slam behind us. Everyone looked at me as Danielle and I made our way through the living room. Mike touched his hand to my shoulder as I passed him.

We formed a circle in the room around Dad, all of us holding hands as Matt said a prayer for Dad and for all of us. I could hear the sniffling of everyone crying, and then I could feel my own tears begin to form behind my eyes. I stared at my feet as I loosely held the hands at my sides. I didn't want to cry, not in front of my dad.

"Oh, Lord, please help the DeJong family in this hard time," Matt began.

When I looked up, my mom was staring at Dad, her eyes fixed right on his, with a sad expression on her face and tears slowly rolling down her cheeks. I tried to make myself look at him, but I just couldn't. The life in his eyes was gone, and his body was still, just lying there.

After Matt finished the prayer, he, my mom, and Beth stayed behind in the room as the rest of us left. Everybody reassembled into the same positions as before: Claire, Tate, and Mitchell sat on the couch, and Emma and Mike stood next to it. I looked at Danielle and motioned towards the front door, and she nodded.

"You know what's weird?" I said as we began to slowly walk down the street.

"What?"

"My mom is a single parent. She's a widow now. You know, she could marry another guy and be married to him longer than she was to my dad."

"Mary."

"No, I'm serious," I told her as I waved my hands to brush off her attempt to quiet me. "There are tons of things I've thought about like that. Like, who will walk me down the aisle when I get married? That is, if I get married."

"You'll get married."

"Oh yeah? To who?"

"To Jake." She smiled at me, and we both laughed. I wiped the tears from my cheeks and looked up at the sky. People from school had teased me a million times about marrying Jake, and I always replied with the same answer.

With a smile on my face I said, "Nah, he's too short."

NOVEMBER 20, 2003

Here is the latest news that we found out this week in Minneapolis.

Monday, we had a CT scan and a PET scan. Tuesday, we met with the doctors to discuss the results. Basically, there is improvement from the last time. The spots on the lungs have shrunk enough that it is hard to distinguish what they are. The tumor in the pelvic area still showed some activity, but not as much as in previous tests. Therefore, on Wednesday, we underwent the procedure to take more biopsies and insert more acetic acid into the active part of the tumor. After eleven biopsies, each showing no active cells, the doctor decided that this was enough. At the angle he was working from, he could not do any more. He said they would look at the biopsies in more detail and let us know on Monday what they find. Based on the outcome, he wants us to come back in a couple of weeks. The outcome is either that they find active cells, and he would insert the acetic acid into those areas, or they do not find any active cells, and he wants to take more biopsies from the anterior (stomach side). He is very excited about the outcome and wants to make sure there is no activity. We asked about the PET scan and why it would show activity. His reply was that with the procedures they are performing, one of the downsides is that they can be deceiving and show activity when there is not. He is hoping that this is the case.

The doctors are also recommending two more rounds of chemo if I can continue to handle the side effects. They do think I am near the end of this chemo drug because of the side effects. We asked the oncologist about this, and he was quick to answer that if we need more chemo treatments, there are three other drugs (one not approved yet but will be soon) that we can switch to. We will schedule these based on the biopsy results.

We have also learned that when we first went to the University of Minnesota and discussed our situation, the doctors met with each other and concluded that this was a complex/complicated case. They are all very interested in the case to see what is going to happen, especially with the pelvic tumor. The acetic acid procedure is fairly new technology. The doctors and nurses are starting to recognize us, and we do not have to explain what is happening each time we meet.

They have even taken it upon themselves to meet with oncology surgeons to discuss the possibility of surgery to remove the mass in the pelvic area along with some of the spots on the lungs that they have mapped out from previous tests. They are discussing this as a preventive measure since the progress has been good. They were previously not in favor of surgery unless the primary site in the pelvic area was controlled. Since things are progressing well, they want to make sure they go the distance to cure this. It is good to know that we are not just another patient, and they see good hope for us.

We are forever thankful for all the thoughts, prayers, support, and good deeds that everyone continues to provide. It may seem insignificant to you, but to us, it is significant and hard to quantify.

Tom

"Get the girl, get the girl!"

I stopped dead in my tracks. "The girl has a name, you know."

I was in sixth grade gym class playing basketball against some of the boys in my class. Since I was the only girl on the court with them, they didn't find it necessary to use my actual name, but instead my gender as a means of identification.

"Don't let her shoot on you, Nate," one of the boys called to my friend who was guarding me. I cut and drove by him for an easy layup.

I looked at him and smiled. "Yeah, Nate. Don't let her shoot on you." His cheeks flushed, and he quickly looked away from me in embarrassment.

I ran back to half-court where I turned around to start playing defense. If I was playing a real game, like I do on my traveling basketball team, I would be much more physical, using my hands and pushing my way through other players to get into position. But in gym class, against boys, I had to be careful where to draw the line. If I put my hands on a boy, even if it was just to play good defense, I might get a few strange looks.

Nate began running toward me after he threw the ball inbounds. He's taller than me, which is rare. I was tall for a girl, and most boys hadn't caught up yet. Nate had blonde hair, a huge smile, and tanned skin that looked even darker because of the bright green cast he had on his arm after breaking his wrist.

"Sorry, I didn't mean to embarrass you," I teased him. "You just make it so easy." He shot a smile at me in response. Nate and I had been in and out of each other's classes for a few years, so he and I were close enough friends that it was okay to make fun of him. He knew I was only kidding.

"Yeah, yeah. Just know that it's not going to happen again," he warned. I laughed at his confidence.

My teammate passed the ball inbounds to me to take up the court. I began dribbling and looking for an open person to hand it off to when I noticed Nate on a full-out sprint heading towards me. A little confused, I dribbled faster down the court to avoid whatever he was planning, where I met another defender. I backed up a few steps to create space and then began to take off to the right, parallel to the sideline.

Distracted by the defender, I hadn't noticed Nate waiting for me behind him. In an attempt to cut across him and go left, my right foot kicked his, tripping both of us. I began to fall forward toward Nate, so I threw the ball outward to another teammate, hoping it would make it all the way there without forcing a turnover. Nate landed flat on his back, his head hitting the metal pole that ran along the length of the dividing curtain, *which was there to keep the curtain from whipping around or moving out of its place.*

It did not take long to realize there was no way of avoiding landing directly on top of Nate's body. Forcing myself to at least fall on him sideways so my head would not land on his, our stomachs were the first to connect. He let out a loud grunt as the weight of my body and the force behind my fall took the air out of his lungs. My chest came downward straight towards his outstretched arm; my collarbone connected with the cast on his wrist, making a "crunch" that was loud enough to stop the basketball game that was still going on around us.

I quickly stood up so I did not have to lie across his body any longer than I needed to, and he did the same. I looked at his face to see if he was all right, and as he started to rub the back of his head where he had hit the metal pole, I began to feel a horrible, aching pain coming from my collarbone where I had hit his cast. I began to slowly realize that even moving my fingers on my right arm was causing extreme pain.

As I could feel tears welling up behind my eyes, I turned towards the door and headed out of the gym to find a teacher and to prevent those boys from seeing me cry.

The only teacher in the gym office was Mr. Webb, who was not my teacher and did not know who I was. "Mr. Webb?" I said, trying to hold back the tears that were beginning to fall against my will. He looked up at me with a concerned look on his face. "I'm in Mrs. Schneider's class. I fell playing basketball, and my bone hit a boy's cast. And now it hurts to move my arm."

"Oh, my," he said as he jumped up from his seat and led me out towards the main office of the middle school. "You'll need to call one of your parents to come get you to take you to the doctor for an x-ray."

He led me down the main hallway by the gyms and the locker rooms until we were out in the commons. I said thank you and began to make my way to the office.

"Hello, this is Mary DeJong. Is Tom DeJong there?" My mom was usually home, but of course on the day that I needed her, she was substitute teaching at an elementary school in town.

I waited for a few seconds before I heard the other line click. "This is Tom," my dad said cheerfully from the other line.

"Hey, Dad. It's me. I was playing basketball in gym class, and I think I broke my bone." I began to cry as I told him what had just happened.

"Oh, kiddo. Mom's subbing today, isn't she?" I could tell he was thinking of how he was going to leave work to come get me. "Can you sit in the office for a few minutes? I'll come as fast as I can, but I need to stop at home first. Is that okay?" I let out an "mhmm" through my tears.

I hung up the phone and went and sat down at one of the chairs lining the inside of the office. I looked down at myself to see that I was still in my gym clothes: a pair of blue mesh basketball shorts, a white t-shirt, and tennis shoes. My face was probably all red and blotchy because of my crying, and I was still sweating from the basketball game. Lovely. All I could do was hope that Dad would hurry, and that no one I knew would come down to the office between now and when he came.

After about forty-five minutes had passed, the secretaries began to shoot me looks of confusion and concern. "What time did he say he was coming?" they would ask me. "Is he coming soon?" I just nodded in response, even though I had no idea when he would show up.

By the time an hour had passed, I was standing up and leaning against the window, watching the loop outside the school to see when Dad's Jeep would come around the corner into sight.

Out of nowhere, the 1987 Jeep Cherokee appeared. I had never seen him take a corner like that; he clearly knew he had kept me waiting for quite some time. I turned to the secretaries behind their desks. "He's here," I told them. They smiled at me in response. "Go get better," the lady at the front desk told me.

I hadn't considered that it was winter, too cold outside for shorts and a t-shirt. As I made my way to the Jeep, my dad jumped out of the driver's door and ran towards me. "I'm so sorry, kiddo. I needed to go home to change my pouch."

"It's okay, Dad."

He led me to the passenger door and helped me into the Jeep. After positioning himself into the seat next to me, he fastened his seat belt and placed his left hand on the very top of the steering wheel, fingers curled downwards. He looked at me and began to laugh. I had no idea what was so funny.

"What are you laughing at?" I asked him.

"You." His shoulders bounced up and down as he laughed. "You're sweating and wearing shorts and a t-shirt. You must be freezing."

"I'm glad that's so funny," I shot at him. "Can we go, please?" I took my left index finger and began to twirl it in a circle, indicating that he needed to move a little faster.

"Yes, yes, I'm going."

Getting in position for the x-rays was one of the most painful experiences of my life. Putting my shoulders straight back to the wall against the will of my broken bone was excruciating.

"We'll call Mom at her school when we get home, okay, kiddo?" Dad said to me as we made our way to the Jeep in the parking lot of the clinic. I turned to him and nodded.

"The doctor told me when you were getting your x-rays done that the cast you'll need to wear will be a soft and cushiony strap that will be tight against your shoulders to pull them back, so your bones will heal straight." He was using his hands to demonstrate how the bones would heal as he described it. "They need to order one for your size, though. So Mom can come pick *that up tomorrow," he explained to me.*

"What do I do until then?" I asked him.

"Be careful, I suppose."

"How long until I can play basketball again?"

"Probably just a few weeks. You'll want to make sure it heals all the way first. You don't want to rush it."

I considered what it would mean to miss a few weeks of basketball as we climbed into our seats of the Jeep. Would I be able to start when I got back? Would my coaches be mad? I mean, I was playing basketball when I got hurt, so it wasn't like I was doing something stupid. I looked up to see that he was staring at me with a huge grin on his face.

"What?"

"Where do you want your ice cream from?"

MAY 20, 2004

We have once again returned from another checkup from Minneapolis after a two-month layoff.

To make a long story short (all kinds of scheduling problems), the doctor on Monday did not have test results to share with us at the time we met. He said that the blood counts looked good and that physically I looked good. Therefore, he did not think there would be any problems. Since we were having another procedure to the pelvic area done on Tuesday, he explained that if something came up, he would find us. We never heard from him again, so we have another two months of no treatments! My health status is as good (maybe better, but we don't know for sure) as it was from our last checkup. I am actually feeling a little better each day.

Tuesday's treatment went well. Instead of using acetic acid, they went into the artery that feeds the tumor (at least the majority of the tumor) and injected a chemo drug into the artery. This will supposedly kill the tumor tissue that is still left. This doctor indicated that the PET scan did show some activity in the pelvic area and a couple of spots on the lungs, which is an improvement to both sites. After the procedure, he felt the coverage was good but found that there is another artery feeding the tumor in the pelvic area. That means they will repeat this procedure in two months if there are any signs of activity. This artery also feeds down into the butt area, so they would have to put a block on that part of the artery before doing the injection. I am really hoping the tests show no signs of activity. I am interested in the procedure, but I don't need to experience it firsthand to find out about it.

That is it for now. This is one of the first times that the doctor on Monday has shown any sign of optimism, so we are feeling pretty good. We still remind ourselves that we are not cured, but maybe things are getting better.

Like I indicated earlier, things get a little better each day, with the emphasis on little. Patience is a virtue.

Tom

MAY 21, 2004

Just when you think life is starting to get a little better, the phone rings. I thought I had waited long enough before I sent you the message yesterday. But our doctor called and had the test results. There are some spots on the lungs (he didn't say how many) that showed some signs of growing. Because of this, he wants to start the chemo treatments again. He did not say how many cycles of treatments in all, but he wants to complete two cycles before our next checkup. He wants to use a drug I have used before in conjunction with a new drug that is supposed to increase the vulnerability of the cancer cells. I will more than likely lose the hair again. Yes, I know what you guys are thinking!

Treatments will probably begin soon. We are doing okay because this is what we were expecting when we went down to Minneapolis. They are very hopeful, but since I am the first person they are doing this type of treatment to, they have no previous results to base anything on. I am doing some physical therapy with some improvement each day. We will just keep plugging away.

Our summer plans are changing every day, but we are still very hopeful. Thanks for everyone's continued support.

Tom

CHAPTER 4

SWOOSH.

"Does that make another win for the home team?" I looked over at Jamison and Emma sitting on the ground, a victorious grin plastered on my face. I had just beaten Jake in the final battle of our Everlasting Lightning game — the two of them had gotten out a while ago.

"Let's do something else," Emma said, ignoring my comment and looking away from the glare of the setting sun.

I looked at the boys now sitting next to each other on the swing and then up at the hoop. "Like what?"

"I don't know," she sighed. "Just not basketball. We could play kick-the-can or something. Or even go inside to play cards."

I felt that lump begin to re-form. "I don't want to go inside."

"Okay, Miss Drama Queen," Emma said in her mocking voice. "Good thing kick-the-can is outside." At this point, we hadn't told the boys about the night's events. Not only did I not want them to act differently, but it never really came up in our conversations.

Jake walked into our garage to grab an empty can out of the recycle bin to place in the center of the driveway to begin our game. As he was searching through the milk cartons and glass jars, the sound of a dog running over to us caught my attention.

"Hey, Skippy," Jamison said as he mustered enough energy to stand up from the swing and greet the dog.

Emma looked at Jake's approaching dad, Rich, and smiled. "Hey, Rich. What's up?"

"Just taking Skippy out for a walk. Poor guy's been tied up all day in the backyard watching you guys run around, and I thought it was his turn for some exercise."

Emma smiled at the dog and then stood up, making her way towards the house.

Rich turned to face me. "So how's Dad doing tonight?"

I cocked my head to the side, not exactly sure of the right way to tell people that your father just died a few minutes ago. "Actually, about an hour or so ago . . . " I nodded my head at him with a that's-too-bad expression as I trailed off, hoping he would understand where I was going with this.

"Oh," he looked down at the ground and then back up at me again. Looking me directly in the eyes he added, "I'm so sorry."

Without knowing how to respond to this, either, I said, "No, that's okay. We were kind of expecting it."

He gave me a half smile as he nodded his head and then looked over at Jake, who had been standing there listening with an empty soup can in his hand. "Jacob, maybe you and Jamison should come to our house and let the girls be with their family tonight."

"No, really, that's alright," I protested. "Mom's inside with my aunt and her family. If Jake and Jamison left, I'd probably still be shooting out here anyway."

Rich considered this and looked back at Jake. "Well," he smiled, "they can only stay if I'm allowed to play one game."

"Hey, you gotta take it up with Emma. She has it in her head that we're supposed to play something besides basketball."

"Mary, you like kick-the-can," Jake said, standing up for Emma, who had temporarily gone inside the house.

"Yes, but that doesn't mean I don't want to play basketball."

"Tell me more about this kick-the-can game," Rich said, with a boyish smile on his face.

I knew Rich liked to play games with us, but I also knew that Rich was only playing so if someone from my family came outside, he would be there to tell Jake and Jamison it was time to go. I didn't mind, though. As normal as he could make this night, the better.

Our house was filled with booklets, pamphlets, and instructional papers letting us know what to expect from a person dying from certain cancers and how to react to things that he or she may say. What these booklets failed to tell us was how to respond to people asking if they can bring you food, or what to say when someone apologizes for the death of your parent. They didn't kill my dad, so why were they saying "sorry" to me?

I ran inside to find Emma. "We're going to start, and you can't play if you come out after we've started."

"I'm coming, I'm coming. Just calm down."

When I ran back outside, my grandparents' car had pulled in front of our driveway. My dad's parents and his two brothers, Rick and Steve, filed out of the car. "Mary," my grandpa said as he nodded, greeting me with a serious expression, but not stopping his slow walk up the driveway. My grandma walked over to me and hugged me. Then without saying a word, she let go and followed Grandpa and my uncles, making her way to the house to say goodbye to her youngest son.

I looked over at Rich, who was watching my expression to see if the game was still a go. I nodded at Jake to put the can on the ground, and Jamison jumped to his feet. "Let's do this."

APRIL 25, 2005

Well, I like it when Tom writes these updates and I just have to forward them. Before I start I will say that he is recovering nicely, so that you don't have to worry about that while reading this. I always appreciate doctors that give us the bottom line before going into all the details.

This chapter starts about three weeks ago. In order to reduce the growth and pain of the pelvic tumor, the doctors decided to have Tom go through about fifteen treatments of radiation. During the first week he got the flu. This didn't seem fair, but many, many people had the flu, so he dealt with it. He got better over the weekend. During the second week of radiation he had a relapse of the flu. This time when we saw the doctor he was told to take an anti-nausea medicine (we have many varieties at home). This worked great, and he was back at work on Friday.

Friday night we left for Arkansas to see my mom, and then he was supposed to spend the week in Kansas City for a business training session. About two hours down the road he realized he had forgotten his anti-nausea medicine - oops! He was pretty uncomfortable on Sunday, but we figured after making several phone calls on Monday and getting his prescription transferred that he would bounce back again like before - wrong. He never made it to Kansas City, and on Thursday we headed for home so that we could get him to the doctor on Friday. (I had to drive the entire thirteen-hour trip — in heavy rain all the way — from Kansas City to Sioux Falls, and I hit a chicken. Any sympathy for me? Just thought I'd try.)

We got home at 2:00 am, and by 5:00 am, we were at the emergency room. After many hours of waiting, what we found out was that from his surgery many years ago, a small loop of his small intestine had fallen down into his pelvic area. When the radiation was shot there, it hardened the stool to a cement-like consistency, thus allowing nothing to pass through. On Saturday around 11:00 am, Tom had surgery to remove the bad part of the colon, and the doctor was able to stitch the rest back together. We had planned on a second colostomy, which was a huge possibility.

He will be in the hospital for three to five days or until things start working properly. He has been pretty groggy, but at least now he is on the side of getting better each day. Needless to say, he never had the flu. We feel fortunate that God got us to the hospital in Fargo and that the correct diagnosis has been made. It is comforting to know that God is with us at every corner. We always feel His comforting touch and presence.

Thank you for your support and God bless all of you.

Tom, Becky, Emma, Mary, and Claire

JUNE 29, 2005

Hello everyone!

I just wanted to tell all of you thank you for all that you have done for us. This last weekend showed how much you care for my family and me. Your actions make me feel that you care for us as if we were one of your children. This love and kindness help to keep me going during the days when I am not feeling so good. There are times when I feel depressed and want to give up and stop treatments, and then I think of my family, all of you, my friends, and the support you have all given, and this gives me the encouragement to keep going.

Thanks again for all that you have done.

Tom

It was hot outside on Sports Day in Iroquois, South Dakota. We were waiting for our family to gather together following the parade we had just watched before heading to go get barbecue for lunch with the rest of the town, and I was sitting on the curb, people-watching.

Iroquois was a small town that has always fascinated me. It was where my dad grew up and went to high school, and every building in the town was old and appeared to be falling apart, but each hinted at a full history years before even my parents were born. I knew I could never stand living in a small town this size, but that didn't stop me from absolutely loving this place.

The dirt and dust blew around in the heat of the day, the windows of the buildings on the main street were often cracked or broken, and I could see the grain elevators by the highway from where I sat on the curb. My favorite place to visit in Iroquois was Dad's high school. There was a small trophy room connected to the old gym where he used to play basketball, and in the trophy room was a black-and-white picture of Dad's young football team. I loved it.

"Ready to go, kiddo?" Dad asked me. He was holding his hand out towards me, offering to help me up from the ground.

"Yeah, I'm starving."

I walked next to Dad on the way to the barbecue place, Mom followed walking next to Grandma, and Emma and Claire walked alongside Grandpa with a few of our cousins.

After we finished eating, Mom was packing up her things to head back to Grandma and Grandpa's house. I listened as Dad told her he was going to stay behind for the day to catch up with some of his high school friends that he hadn't seen in years.

"Can I stay with you?" I asked him.

"I don't know." He was looking at my mom instead of me. "I'm probably going to be here until later tonight, and there won't be a ride back for you if you want to leave earlier."

"That's okay. I want to stay." Now I was looking at Mom too.

She could tell that we were asking her for permission, rather than actually discussing with each other if it was a good idea or not, and she smiled and rolled her eyes at the two of us.

"You can stay with Dad, but like he said, you have to stay the whole time." I nodded in response.

Several hours after the sun had set, there was a street dance taking place on the same street where the parade had gone down hours before. There was a DJ set up playing loud music, people were outside drinking and dancing, and there were lights set up surrounding the entire area.

"I'm glad we live in a bigger city than this," I told Dad as we were walking on the sidewalk next to the crowd of people, "but I think this would be a fun part of living in a small town."

"It is," he said. "They didn't have a lot of street dances when I was growing up, but we had events like this that we loved going to. I always played in the softball tournaments they had every summer."

We got to the entrance of a small bar. The building had dark wood siding and small windows that displayed neon signs advertising different kinds of alcohol. There was music, loud *laughter, and smoke billowing out the front propped-open door. Dad walked in, and I paused at the doorway.*

"Dad?" He turned around to face me. "I can't go in here."

He laughed at what I was saying. "Another perk of a small town: they won't serve you any alcohol, but you can definitely come in a bar with me."

I was nervous. I had never even been near a bar before. My parents didn't drink or smoke, and this was a crowd of people unlike anyone we spent time with at home. I walked closely behind Dad as he made his way through the crowded bar towards a table with his friends from high school.

I took a seat next to Dad and sat there, nervous and people-watching. He leaned close to me and pointed at each person as he told me their names: Kathy, Tony, Doug, and Mike. Each gave a small wave and a closed-mouth smile as he said their names. I quietly said, "hi," and then they continued the conversation they were having before we sat down.

I thought of Emma and Claire playing the Nintendo in Grandma's basement and how much fun that sounded right now. Shoot. I needed to pretend to not be miserable because Dad warned me I would be here with him for a long time without a ride back, and I didn't want him to have to take care of me or leave his friends.

My attention was broken as the woman sitting on the other side of me, Kathy, started to talk to me. She was leaning in close so I could hear her; her face was only a few inches away from mine, and she was smiling as she spoke. "Did you know that your dad was so smart in high school that we used to call him 'Computer Head'?" I smiled and shook my head at her.

"We had a substitute teacher in math class one day," she continued, "and she wasn't teaching the lesson correctly, according to your dad. So, politely, he raised his hand and offered to take over." She started to laugh as she recounted

her high school memories. "He actually taught our math class that day."

"Oh, we're telling Tom's daughter stories about him from high school?" Doug, across the table, had apparently heard what Kathy was telling me and wanted to join the conversation. "This oughta be fun."

"Oh, boy," Dad said as he leaned back in his chair.

"Remember the time when you'd had so much to drink that you couldn't find your car keys to go home, so you spent the night sleeping in the bed of your white pickup? And in the morning, you woke up to find that the keys had been in the bed of the pickup with you the entire time?" The table erupted with laughter. I looked at my dad, astonished that this was a true story from his high school days.

"I don't actually," he answered laughing, his shoulders bouncing up and down. "But I suppose that makes sense considering the story." He rubbed his eyes with his hands. Behind where we sat, I heard a loud crashing sound, followed by several people laughing and cheering. I figured these must be ordinary bar sounds because no one at the table even turned around to see where the crash had come from.

My uncle Steve appeared behind me and came to stand next to the table. "When we were kids," he began, "we used to line up ketchup packets along the side of the highway, and we would ride our bikes over them, so they would squirt ketchup everywhere." He smiled at the thought of his own story. "The things that used to entertain us."

The table continued to tell stories, but I started to look around the bar, now much more comfortable with my surroundings considering I had been there for a little while. Looking down at the table in front of Dad, I realized that he had a brown drink in a clear plastic cup in front of him. I had never seen my dad drink before, except after his softball games in the gravel parking lots behind the fields. Emma and I used to step on the team's empty beer cans so they would curl over our shoes, and then we would walk around with them on our feet.

"Want a drink?" he asked me as he pushed the cup in my direction. He had clearly seen me eyeing his cup. He waited for me to grab the cup, but I didn't move. "It's just Diet Coke," he said, aware that I was thinking it was an alcoholic drink. He looked at me a little closer and studied my eyes. "Do your eyes sting? Because of the smoke?" A little embarrassed, I nodded. He leaned in even more so his mouth was almost touching my ear. "Mine too. I hate being in smoky bars."

CHAPTER 5

"HELLO? YES, THANK YOU. WE'RE hanging in there. Yes, it's very hard. Okay. All right. Wednesday? We should be around. Oh, that would be great. Thanks so much. Okay, bye." It was yet another conversation with a family friend of some sort or a member of our church. Everyone called to tell us how sorry they were, to offer their condolences, and to suggest they bring food over to us. I had to admit, it wasn't awful going into the kitchen with an empty stomach, only to find that the refrigerator was jam-packed with casseroles, pastas, breads, fruit dishes, salads, and desserts. There were always containers of cookies or homemade bars to be found lying around the house, and empty Tupperware waiting for its owner to retrieve it.

"Who was that?" Emma asked excitedly. "What are they bringing?"

"Church people, Emma. And soup."

Claire and I were sitting on the couch finishing our lunch when we heard cars honking outside, loud and obnoxious.

My mom put her head down and sighed. "Oh, boy."

Emma ran to the door. "Mom, it's Dave!" My mom's college friends had all met and now created a small parade of cars down our street, complete with honking and waving.

We put down our plates where we could find space in the unusual clutter of our house, and ventured outside to see who had just arrived. Waiting with open arms was my mom's best friend from college, Dave. Dave was a large, bald man with a dry and sarcastic sense of humor. Just listening to the comments he would make could keep anyone laughing.

"Hey, Becky. How are you holding up?" he asked as Mom let him wrap his arms around her.

"As well as we can," she looked at me and smiled. "I think we're doing okay."

"Here, we brought you a tree." Holding a medium-sized pine tree in one hand was Scott, another college friend.

Scott beamed. But my mom looked confused and glanced back and forth between the two men. "A tree, huh? What's that for?"

"Well, it's for you!" Dave said, pointing a finger at us. "We figured you could plant it in your backyard as sort of an in-memory-of kind of thing. What do you think?"

"Well, it's interesting."

Emma chimed in. "I think it's cool. When do we plant it?"

"Right now works for me," Scott said, already welcoming himself through our garage to the backyard. As we followed him, I noticed the rest of Mom's college friends were getting out of their cars to join us.

They all walked to the back and stood around looking at each other, realizing that they hadn't thought of their next step: how they were going to get the tree into the ground.

"So, Becky," Rich, another one of her friends, said as he looked around the yard, "do you have any shovels?"

My mom laughed, shook her head, and headed back into the garage.

As they began to dig up the ground, my mom leaned in close to me and whispered, "My purse is in the kitchen. In my purse is my camera. I need you to go get that camera." I heard Claire giggling behind me, and I turned around to run inside.

Once the tree was planted, Scott disappeared into his car and reappeared with a case of Mike's Hard Lemonade. "Shall we?" he said.

Everyone circled around the new addition to our yard. Dave held up one of the bottles. "To Tom," he said and took a drink. He let out a sharp exhale and handed the bottle to Dan on his left. He didn't say anything, but he kept a serious face and held the bottle in the air, still looking at the tree. After a few seconds, he took a drink and then continued the passing of the bottle.

Toward the end of the circle stood my sisters and me. When the bottle came to the first of us, ten-year-old Claire, she looked at the bottle and then looked at the rest of the group with an expression that asked if she was actually supposed to continue the process. My mom came and took the bottle from her and said, "Let's water the tree." I laughed, thinking she was kidding, and she said, "I love you, Tom. I always will," and she poured a small amount of the spiked lemonade onto the ground at the base of the tree.

She looked at Claire and held up the bottle, raising her eyebrows to encourage her to join in. Claire followed cue saying, "I love you too, Daddy," and poured a couple more drops onto the ground. It was very clear that she wanted to smile at the fact that she just watered a tree planted for her deceased father with alcohol, but she knew this was supposed to be moderately serious. Doing her best not to let the corners of her mouth curl into a smile, she quickly turned, handed Emma the bottle, and turned back, looked at the ground, and held her hands together.

"Well, she doesn't have a fever," Mom said as I pulled the covers of my parents' bed up to my chin. Mom and Dad were

both standing next to the bed, Mom dressed to go sub at a nearby elementary school and Dad dressed for work.

"I know I don't have a fever," I told her. "I have a really bad stomachache."

"You really shouldn't miss school." I could see her thinking about all of the possibilities of what might come of today. I imagined she was wondering who would stay home with me if they both had to work today. Dad had his job, and Mom had already committed to subbing. She looked at Dad, and I watched as they had a silent conversation through their facial expressions.

"I can stay home with her," Dad finally said out loud.

Mom considered this. "But only if she goes to the doctor," she said. Then she looked at me. "Are you sick enough that you need to go to the doctor?"

I nodded. "It really hurts."

"I'll go call the office," Dad said as he limped out of the room, his cane in his right hand. I could hear the rubber on the tip of his cane thump on the floor as he made his way down the hallway toward the kitchen. Mom stayed behind and looked at me with a concerned expression. She walked toward me and sat on the edge of the bed, and she put her hand on my stomach, gently rubbing it.

"I'm sorry you don't feel very well," she said. "Are you missing anything important today at school?" I shrugged, and she said, "I wish I could stay, but I need to get going. Dad will be with you today, and then I'll be home around four o'clock this afternoon." She leaned down, kissed me on the forehead, and headed out of their bedroom.

Dad met her at the door. "All set. I'll have to do some work from home today, but I'm covered for any meetings planned at the office." He looked over at me. "Okay, kiddo. Why don't you get up so we can head to the clinic to get that stomach of yours checked out?"

The children's walk-in clinic was decorated with sculptures of a giant mouse and balloons. I thought it was really babyish, and I could only imagine how "children" who were sixteen or seventeen felt about coming here. At least I was still sort of a kid since I was in middle school.

"How are you feeling right now?" Dad asked as he looked at me over the Sports Illustrated magazine he had picked up from an end table next to the waiting room chairs.

"I'm fine. Stomach just hurts. It feels really crampy." He furrowed his eyebrows to show concern and then nodded while directing his attention back to the sports article he was reading.

The smell of this clinic was stale, like the smell of the hospital. I was used to going to the hospital all the time. It was almost like a second home to me. I'd had countless meals, sleepovers, and hours spent doing homework there. This clinic, though, wasn't a place I was used to being.

"Mary?" In the doorway that led back to the small meeting rooms stood a nurse holding a clipboard and propping the wooden door open with her back. When she saw me look up at the sound of my name, she smiled at me and said, "You can follow me this way. Dad can come too if he wants."

Several minutes later I found myself lying on a cold, hard, and narrow blue "bed" with the doctor sitting next to me on a stool with wheels. He had a white mask over his mouth and an instrument in his hand to rub on my stomach to see what was going on inside that was causing me pain.

"Feels backwards, doesn't it?" Dad said with a smile on his face. "I'm usually the one in a bed with you sitting next to me." We both laughed, but the doctor didn't seem to think that was all that funny.

Without warning, what felt like a smooth block of ice was rubbing on my stomach. It made me gasp and quickly suck in my stomach to get away from what was causing that feeling.

"It's okay," the doctor said. "It's just me doing the ultrasound. This machine is like a camera, and that screen will show me what is inside your stomach." As he spoke, he pointed to what looked like a TV screen.

"This is also how they see inside the stomachs of women who are pregnant," Dad explained. When I looked over at him, he was smiling as if he was about to make one of his jokes. "Any surprises we should be waiting for?"

"What?" I shouted at him. "No, obviously not! Jeez." Again, what we thought was funny wasn't shared by the doctor.

When we were finished at the clinic, we climbed back into Dad's Jeep to head to the pharmacy. This North Dakota winter hadn't been friendly, so even though it was finally beginning to feel like spring outside, we didn't waste any time closing the doors and turning up what little heat the Jeep could muster.

"Well, since you're just constipated, I guess you're not really sick," Dad said with almost too much enthusiasm.

"Dad, holy. That's really gross."

"We need to go pick up your laxative, but then let's go out for lunch. What do you feel like? Ground Round for some cheeseburgers? I'm sure they're showing the March Madness games on the TVs there."

I smiled at the idea and nodded. "Will Mom be mad? She'd probably send me back to school if she was here with me instead of you."

"A little hooky never hurt anyone," he said as he started to pull out of the parking lot. "Especially since Duke plays this afternoon."

"Okay," I agreed, "but can you not use the word 'laxative' so freely? It's like you don't have a filter." He only laughed, which wasn't really a comforting answer to my request.

We stayed at Ground Round for about two hours eating cheeseburgers and watching the college basketball games. When we got home, the temperature had started to warm up, and our driveway looked more inviting to us than our empty house.

"What do you think?" I asked him. "Want to shoot some hoops?"

He smiled at me. "It's like you read my mind. It'll feel good to move after sitting for a few hours."

I ran inside the garage to grab my basketball from the rack on the wall, and Dad limped towards the base of the hoop.

"You shoot, and I'll rebound," he said. I dribbled the ball towards the basketball hoop until I was within a comfortable shooting range, and I took my first shot. It bounced off the side of the rim, and Dad half limped and half jogged over to the ball while holding his cane under his arm. He grabbed the ball from the grass where it had stopped and threw it back to me. "More arch," he said.

The second the ball hit my fingertips, I squared up and let the ball fly. It made the sound every basketball player loves to hear: the snap of the net as the ball falls through the center of the rim. "There ya go," he said as he rebounded by pushing the ball back towards my direction with the end of his cane.

After a few minutes, he grabbed the ball but didn't throw it back. I stood there with my hands up, ready for the ball that wasn't coming my way. With the ball under his arm, he headed in the direction of his Jeep. When I realized he was going to his sweet spot by the driver's door, the shot he always nailed when he would come home from work in the summertime, I smiled and ran to the base of the hoop to catch his rebound. He got himself in position, propped his cane up against the door of the Jeep, and took his shot. The ball flew with a perfect spiral towards the basket, and out of habit, I got into rebounding position — as if there was any defense around to challenge me. Barely too strong, the ball hit the far side of the rim and, bouncing high in the air, headed toward the street.

I ran to go grab it in an attempt to stop it before it left the driveway, but it was unavoidable. I followed the ball, and in the middle of the street, I grabbed it. I looked up just in time to see Mom's minivan as it rounded the corner heading home. "Shoot," I muttered to myself. I dribbled the ball back towards Dad, who was still standing in his sweet spot and staring at the rim, wondering what went wrong with his shot to make him miss.

"Mom's home," I said.

"She is? Where are your sisters? They should have beaten her home."

"Claire has some after-school club today, and Emma has a choir thing, I think."

Before he could respond, the sound of Mom's tires rolling over the curb on the end of the driveway caused us to turn around. I nervously waved at her and walked to the side of the driveway to make way for the van to find its spot in the garage. Once she parked, I walked towards Dad to wait and greet her, the ball still held on my hip under my arm. I looked at Dad to see him giving me a guilty smile.

"Uh-oh," he said. "I think we might be in trouble."

OCTOBER 20, 2005

Tom needs your prayers now. I never like writing these updates because it usually means that Tom can't. Right now he is in the hospital recovering from a surgery to clean out a very serious infection in his pelvic region.

Within three weeks, he went from being out of town working, to mentioning a twinge in his leg that caused him to sit down, to not being able to walk at all. The past three weeks have been a blur of activity in which Tom's condition has changed daily. To start, you have to understand that Tom never complains, so when he says that something hurts or is uncomfortable, I listen because it is always much more than that.

Here is brief rundown of Tom's last few weeks: it started with a phone call from Bismarck (9-28-05) when he said he was teaching at a training school, and he had to sit down because his leg didn't feel like it would support him. He returned home, and each day his leg got worse, so he switched from his cane to crutches (10-1-05) so that he didn't need to put any weight on his right leg. By Sunday (10-2-05), I was asking if he could make it to his Tuesday appointment. We called on Monday (10-3-05) to try and get in earlier but went with an early morning x-ray before his appointment with his oncologist. The x-ray (10-4-05) showed something in his hip joint, but we weren't sure what. As the week progressed, I continued to watch Tom lose more and more of his mobility. When we went in on Friday (10-7-05) for his chemo treatment, I talked with the social worker about sending someone to the house to give us advice about safety issues.

He has weekly lab work done, but some of his numbers were way off, so the doctor ordered daily lab work through the weekend. On Sunday (10-9-05) when I returned home from church, he told me that he needed to go to the hospital to have some units of plasma. His blood was too thin, and his body wasn't working fast enough to thicken it up. We spent most of Sunday in the hospital. He hates hospitals.

On Monday (10-10-05) I met with our insurance representative about getting a motorized wheelchair. It looks hopeful, but there is a lot of red tape to

go through. Next, we went to the hospital to have an
MRI done to get a better picture of what was going on
in his pelvic region. Through the next several days
(10-11-05 through 10-14-05) we had visits from a home
health nurse, a physical therapist, an occupational
therapist, and we met with someone about the wheelchair.
Both of our heads were spinning with information
that we hadn't thought we would have to worry about
so quickly. Thank goodness for my sister, who is a
physical therapist, who helped explain the stuff we
didn't understand (or want to understand). During all
of this, he was beginning to have trouble moving his
left leg, and he mentioned a pain on his bottom - alert!

Over the weekend he started spiking fevers. We were
told that we could expect this from his plasma treatment
for as long as two weeks. We just monitored his fever,
which always returned to normal after a while.

On Monday (10-17-05) he was able to try a motorized
wheelchair at home. It was very nice. The girls and I
thought it was fun. Tom didn't get out of bed much to
appreciate it.

On Tuesday (10-18-05) he asked for help with personal
things that he has never asked for help with before. He
had a fever, and I thought he looked yellow. I called
the doctor's office and they said to bring him in at
2:30. Later that morning, we noticed some drainage
from a sore in his pelvic region. Once we got to the
doctor's office, things moved quickly. They did admit
him and start him on strong antibiotics. The sore on
his bottom stumped most of the people that looked at
it. It wasn't a bed sore, and it was in a location
that was very unusual. (Leave it to Tom to make things
interesting.) On Wednesday (10-19-05) a surgeon looked

at the sore and said he needed surgery to drain the infection. The surgery was last night at 9:00.

What I was told was that Tom is in very serious condition. They will repeat the surgery on Friday morning to clean the area further. Right now he has a breathing tube in so that high doses of morphine can be administered to keep him comfortable. The infection is very serious, and the doctor said that he will probably get worse before he gets better and that recovery could take two-three months.

I hope it helps you to know that Tom loves and trusts God. We both know that God has a plan for Tom and for our family. We will follow whatever path God leads us on. We do ask for your prayers. Thank you for your love. We feel that support and strength every day. Without God, family, and friends, we couldn't do this.

In God's name,
TBEMC

"I'm not hungry."

"Tom, you need to eat something," my mom prodded at my dad, who was lying in bed for the third day in a row.

"I don't know, Beck. I'm just not hungry. If I eat, I'll just throw it up."

It was March, and we were in Arkansas visiting Grandma Fidler while the three of us had a weeklong break from school because of teachers' conventions. Grandma had something planned for our family to do each day, but Dad had taken the last three days off and just stayed in bed, unable to keep any food down.

"My stomach feels full," he told my mom. "I know that's impossible because I haven't eaten anything for a few days, but I'm full. And sick."

"Here," she said as she began to dig through her purse. "Eat a protein bar. Just for now."

I was standing outside the room, just far enough away that I could hear what they were saying, but they wouldn't know I was there.

They were quiet for a minute. "I don't know what to do," my mom finally continued. "I don't want to cut the girls' vacation short, but you need to go to the hospital." She paused, thinking of all possible options. "You can't go to the hospital here because I know something is wrong. And we can't stay longer than a few days because the girls need to be home and back at school." I could hear the stress in her voice.

"I'll be okay for a few days," he told her. "Just have fun with the girls, and we'll figure this out when we get home."

"No. It isn't okay that you haven't eaten in days."

I could hear her start walking towards the doorway. I whipped around and ducked inside the bathroom to my left. When I heard her footsteps reaching my grandma's living room, I poked my head into the hallway to see if the coast was clear. I stood up straight and walked back into the room my dad was in.

"Hey, Dad."

"Hey, kiddo," he said as he rolled over onto his side to face me. "What have you been up to today?"

"Emma and I just went on a ride in Grandma's golf cart."

"By yourselves?" He smiled at me. As hard as he tried to hide it, it was all too evident that his smile was forced and unnatural.

"Yep, Grandma said we could." I turned my attention downwards toward my feet. "Dad? Are we leaving early?"

He looked at me and considered if he should tell me the truth or not. I always told my parents that I knew I was young, but I still wanted to know everything that went on with my dad. I didn't want them to keep anything from me or sugarcoat any bad news.

"We'll see," he finally said. "Your mom and I aren't sure what's going on with me."

"Why aren't you hungry? Grandma has a fruit basket out in the kitchen. I can peel an orange or cut up an apple for you if you want."

He smiled a genuine smile at me this time. "Why don't you just come lay with me?"

I walked around to the other side of the bed and did my best to slide under the covers without moving the bed. I didn't want to stir up his stomach any more than it already was.

"Where did you and Emma go with the golf cart?" he asked.

"Just around the neighborhood. I know my way around pretty well. Of course Emma doesn't, but I told her where to go."

He laughed in response. Emma has always been known in my family as incredibly intelligent, but also directionally challenged. She had no idea how to get from Point A to Point B, even if she made that trip every day.

"Tom?" My mom was calling from the kitchen. I could hear her footsteps approaching as she spoke. "I think it's best if we go home in the morning. I know the girls will be disappointed, but they're old enough to understand." She stopped quickly in the doorway when she saw me. She clearly had assumed I was still outside with Emma.

"It's okay, Mom," I said. "I know he needs to go to the hospital."

She made her way around the bed and sat next to where I had my legs fully outstretched. "Well, look at you," she said as she smiled at me. "You're growing up."

"She even knows her way around the winding and twisting roads of Grandma's neighborhood," my dad told her.

"I know," my mom laughed. "Grandma was telling me how she had to direct Emma."

"I'm not that good with directions," I said. "She's just really bad." Dad laughed and looked at Mom, but her attention was gone. She had her eyes set on the deck outside where Claire and Grandma were sitting in the hot tub and playing with the toy ducks.

My dad noticed her distraction and watched her focus her attention outside. "It's okay, Beck," he said. "We'll be home tomorrow."

CHAPTER 6

"COME ON GIRLS, GRANDPA'S BUYING our family dinner tonight at Applebee's," my grandma called to Emma and me downstairs. I wanted to go to dinner with all of our DeJong cousins, but still, I was hesitant to leave the house. All of our family and friends from anywhere and everywhere were showing up that night to see and spend time with us.

When we returned home, we noticed the cards had already begun. Playing cards was considered a sport to both sides of my family, as well as to all of my mom's college friends. There were several tables lined up in a row in the garage, so there was room for all fifteen of the participants.

As our DeJong clan made our way up the driveway to the cards party in the garage, Grandma Fidler ran over to me.

"Mary, who is that cutie Emma's walking with?" Grandma obviously missed the memo that this was a DeJong family meal. "I could see them together."

"Grandma, that's my cousin Mike."

"Oh." She considered this for a moment and then laughed. "I could see him with me."

I looked at her grinning at me from ear to ear. "You're so weird, Grandma."

My mom's approaching friend, Rich, broke my attention.

"So, I hear you've become quite the ball player," he said, hinting at a challenge, my ball under his arm.

"You've heard that, huh?" I grabbed the ball from him. "Well, I don't know about that."

"Hey, it's not like I believed it."

"Oh, really," I said as I nailed an eight-foot jump shot.

"All right, all right, I see you," he said nodding his head and smiling.

I walked up to the edge of the driveway. "Check."

"Woah, home court advantage, my friend. My ball first."

Rolling my eyes at him, I took a few steps forward and turned around, ready to pass him the ball. The instant the ball made contact with his hands, he shot, hoping to score a quick three-pointer. As it bounced off of the very top of the backboard, I reached up and grabbed it, pulled it down, and dribbled out to the top of the key.

I shot him an are-you-kidding-me look as I stood there dribbling, and he threw his hands in the air. "What? I'm a little rusty, that's all."

I faked left and cut right, and he stayed right with me. As he shuffled backwards near the hoop, his foot hit the wooden board that surrounded the outside of the house. His arms began to fly through the air in an attempt to regain his balance, but no matter what he did, he wasn't going to beat gravity. He hit the rocks, scraping the backs of his arms and legs.

At that moment, Dave had looked up from his cards in the garage and saw Rich lying in the rocks. "What did you do to him?" he called out from the garage. "Poor old man."

"I didn't do anything! He just fell."

"Yeah, right," said a struggling Rich, trying to get to his feet.

"You were so frustrated with how badly I was beating you that you grabbed me by the shirt and threw me to the ground."

"Mary," my mom said without looking up from her hand of cards, "don't beat up Rich."

My jaw dropped. I hit the side of Rich's arm. "You're nuts."

OCTOBER 22, 2005

This is my common response when people ask me about Tom: he is doing as well as can be expected.

After the surgery on Wednesday, they put Tom in the ICU. They have him on a ventilator due to high doses of morphine, and they have him in restraints so that he will not pull out the breathing tube. They also have him on a drug that relaxes him and will give him amnesia. The doctors will do what they feel is best, but I have requested that he have as much morphine as he can get and as much Versed as possible so that he will not remember any of this. I feel that until the breathing tube is removed and he can communicate, the less he remembers, the better.

On Friday, he had another procedure done to further clean out his pelvic region. The surgeon said it looked much better and that the infection was starting to clear up. What he found was that there was a leak in his bowel. This leak of stool is what caused the infection. While this is not good news, it is an answer to why the infection was there. They don't yet know what caused the leak: cancerous tumor, weakened bowel from radiation last spring, . . . ? They will do a special x-ray early next week that will help tell where the leak is, maybe what caused it, and hopefully what to do to repair it. Because of the leak he cannot eat any food, so he will be fed through his blood. There are more scientific terms for a lot of these procedures, but my brain converts them into words that I can understand. Hopefully it makes more sense to you that way, too.

Today the surgeon wants to replace the bandages in his wound. They will let this heal as an open wound, which means that it has to heal from the inside out. This is intended to help prevent further abscesses from occurring. Once he is strong enough, he will have another surgery to fix the bowel. Without knowing for sure, I was told Tom will be in the hospital for at least one-two weeks.

I thought it was interesting that, at this point, Tom has four doctors closely monitoring his progress. Nothing that happens to him right now goes unnoticed. He has a surgeon, a critical care doctor, an infectious disease doctor, and his oncologist.

I hope this report doesn't sound too grim because I feel very positive. Throughout Tom's course of treatments, we have been given so many "I don't know what to do" answers. Now I feel like we do know what to do, so we can look to the future for a while. As always, we know who is really in charge.

God Bless,
TBEMC

OCTOBER 27, 2005

I felt like a cheerleader this morning. Oh, I'd better

back up. Yesterday, I was told that the doctors were going to reduce Tom's oxygen level on the ventilator, and then today they would try to let him breathe on his own for a while. When I showed up today I wasn't paying attention until I heard a sound, and I looked over to see Tom's mouth moving. I realized that he was completely off the ventilator!

I had just missed them removing the tube by about ten minutes. His throat is very sore, and his voice is very scratchy. He is also off the morphine drip and Versed. As the day progressed, he began to realize more and more of what was going on around him.

He would like to go home, but that is still a ways off. He wasn't aware that he had been in the hospital for over a week. They will monitor him for twenty-four hours and then move him to the main floor of the hospital.

Keep up the good work! Rah! Rah! Rah! God is listening to your prayers!

Love,
TBEMC

CHAPTER 7

"EMMA, WE'RE GOING TO BE late!" I called downstairs to Emma getting ready in her bathroom, three minutes after we were planning on leaving.

"You said 6:30!" she yelled back up the stairs. "It doesn't start until 7!"

I turned to my mom who was quietly sitting in the living room near where I stood. "Mom, she's always late."

"Yes, Mary. But if she always is, why would she change tonight?"

"Whatever, I'll go shoot outside until she's ready."

"Okay, but don't get mad when you're sweating at the church because you were too impatient to wait for your sister."

I looked at her and then at the door leading to the garage and thought about my options. Sighing, I plopped down on the couch next to my mom. "Dad would make her hurry up."

Instantly I regretted my comment, and Mom gave me a stern look. She must have noticed my regret because she started to smile. "No, he wouldn't. You and I both know he'd be later than her."

I looked at her and laughed. "Yeah, I guess that's true."

"Good evening," Matt began. The congregation was still shuffling behind us, finding their seats while trying to be quiet so we could start the service. "Before we get started," he said, "there are still some seats right up here in the front row for anyone who is standing and would prefer to sit." He paused. "You can tell this is a crowd full of church people because the last row to fill is the front."

He waited for some people to move forward, but no one left their seats in the back of the church. The rest of the rows were filled with people sitting shoulder to shoulder. They were standing along the sides, too, and in the back of the sanctuary.

Matt looked around at the mournful faces staring up at him and decided to begin. "Jesus said, 'Come to me all who are weary and are carrying heavy burdens, and I will give you rest.'"

I looked at Emma to my left as Matt continued the opening of the memorial service. Emma was expressionless, emotionless, and staring forward, directly into the empty space in front of her. She was not looking at Matt, and she was not blinking, but she just sat there with her hands folded in her lap.

To my right were Claire, Mom, and then Beth. In the row directly behind us sat Rick and his family; behind them, Steve and his family. Row by row, my family filled the pews on the left side of the church. Behind my most distant family members sat two rows full of my mom's college friends and their families. I guess I knew that they would probably come, but for some reason I was surprised and truly appreciative of the fact that they all came together to support my family.

"And at this time," Matt continued, "we invite any of you who would like to share a favorite memory of Tom, or offer some sort of tribute, to come forward and do so for the benefit of sharing for all."

The only positive side to this situation was that our family had the benefit of being prepared. We knew what was inevitably going to happen to my dad, and because of this, we were able to plan for this night, as well as the funeral. My mom had sent out an email informing friends and family that there was going to be an opportunity to share memories and stories, and she would like them to prepare short speeches to give.

The first person to approach the podium was Gayle Thostenson. Gayle was from our church, and her family was good friends with my family.

"It is impossible for me to remember Tom anywhere but in the midst of his family," she said. "Perhaps I knew Becky and the girls first, but I think that the reason runs much deeper. For Tom, family was not only his first priority, his greatest love, but it was what kept him going. His girls — you could see the pride in his eyes whenever he spoke about them. Every one of the four was the apple of his eye."

As she continued to recollect and share her memories of my dad, I turned around to look at everyone watching her speak. The phrase "not a dry eye in the house" is, to me, an overused saying to describe sad situations. But as I scanned the faces in the church, person-by-person, I found that there is truth behind that frequently used saying. Every single set of eyes was filled with tears. Some people let the tears run down their cheeks, some wiped them away in an attempt to keep their composure, and some hid their whole faces behind their cupped hands, letting their emotions pour out and seep between their fingers.

I watched as Gayle made her way back to her seat. She had a Kleenex that she was dabbing under her eyes as she walked.

Following Gayle, a man who worked with my dad approached the front of the church. After introducing himself to a crowd who likely did not recognize him, he instantly jumped into describing my dad from a workplace perspective, one that I did not know very well.

"Tom was a humble man," he said. "I doubt he would brag about the great work that he did for us. Girls, I want you to know that your dad was one of the best USDA statisticians in the entire country. His leadership, communication, patience, and all the things that you came to know as a family were also his strengths at work. Tom was the leader of all of us. He came to us with maturity and a level-headedness that kept all of us moving forward and doing a good job."

He listed some of my dad's awards and accomplishments throughout his years at work, and then he finished up with some personal stories before making his way back into the congregation.

I had known that my dad was smart, and that he was looked up to in his field of work. I did not realize that his awards hanging in the computer room of our house were so prestigious and so rarely given. Those awards were a huge honor, and he had never even told me about them. I just sat there in the pew, thinking about how proud I was to be my dad's daughter.

After a short silence, Beth stood up from the front pew next to my mom to head up to the podium.

"I'm Beth Hall, Becky's sister and Tom's card partner," she said. "I was doing okay today until my nieces played his favorite music. Thanks, girls." She paused as she wiped her eyes and took a deep breath. "Wasn't he amazing? I mean, isn't that what you hear? From everyone? Because you all agree with me. So I got to thinking, how can one person be all that to everyone, and so many other people, in all of the areas of his life?

"These past seven years he had the cancer, but it's not *because* he had cancer. Cancer does not define Tom. He lived before cancer, during cancer, and now eternally, he'll be living after cancer."

I could hear her voice tremble as she started to cry, but she kept on talking to the crowd of people, who were so intently holding on to each word she said. "So, why was he so amazing to all of us?" she asked. "It's simple. He lived. He lived in a way that inspired us, made us feel good about ourselves, and brought out the best in us." She took a step back from the podium and looked down at her feet, her eyes shut tight. Still looking down, she raised the microphone to her mouth. "I was lucky. I had conversations with Tom from time to time. He truly, he *truly*, had given his life over to God's plan for him several years ago." She looked up at all the faces staring back at her. "He told me how he had an indescribable peace wash over him. He couldn't even explain it when he had a conversation with God. He gave his life to God.

"He cared about all of us. We are Tom's community. We are connected to each other by having been touched by him, and now this community has a job to do. He asked us to take care of his girls. And you know who I'm talking about: Mary, Claire, Emma, and his first girl, Becky. This community is going to amaze him because I know we won't let him down. I am fortunate to have met many amazing people in my life who bring out the best in me, Tom being one of them. Tom brought out the best in all of us. We liked just being with Tom," she stopped and wiped her eyes with the sleeve of her sweater. She stood up straight and looked out into the pews in front of her. "I am going to cry tomorrow, and I know exactly when I'm going to cry," she said. "It will be when his daughter Claire plays 'Amazing Grace,' and I will be overwhelmed with the loss of our amazing Tom."

She clicked off the microphone and walked from the podium back to her seat next to my mom. She sat down and placed her head onto my mom's shoulder. My mom responded by putting her arm around Beth, and they both sat there and cried. The sanctuary was almost silent, with only the sounds of sniffling and heavy breathing behind me.

NOVEMBER 4, 2005

God is GREAT!

Tom was very nervous about this operation. Until the surgeon was actually operating, there was no way to tell what he was going to find or what the outcome would be. Tom did have several talks with the surgeon prior to the operation that seemed to calm him somewhat.

I was expecting it to be about a four-hour surgery. Dr. Mystery said it went better than he could have expected. The colon had adhered or fused itself to the bone and pelvic wall. He was able to remove the bad part of the colon and attach good colon to good colon. Tom will be in the hospital for at least another week without food to let everything completely heal. They will administer strong antibiotics that will stop any more infection and hopefully clear up the hip joint. There may be future work done to the hip joint, but it is too early to say what that could be, and maybe the drugs will do the trick.

The doctor didn't see any cancer in the intestinal region. He is sending the colon that was removed for testing, and we will know those results later.

I don't think that we could have gotten any better news than we did. Thank you for your prayers and love.

In God's name,
TBEMC

NOVEMBER 12, 2005

Tom is getting stronger every day. He has had no setbacks since I last wrote. Each of the improvements is small, and individually, they don't seem that big, but when they are put together, then it is easy to see how far he has come.

The wound on his bottom is healing fine. The nurse only changes his dressings twice a week. He is no longer running fevers. He has physical therapy every day. His range of motion is increasing, and he can do all the work on his left leg by himself. He can sit up on the edge of the bed by himself and scootch around enough to get himself comfortable. He took four steps forward and four backward yesterday, and he is on clear liquids.

His spirits are amazing. He is doing puzzle books and reading his sports magazines. It took a long time for the morphine to get out of his brain. I think his brain is finally clear enough to concentrate on these activities.

I could keep adding to this list, but as you can see, he is moving in the right direction. We have not been given a release date yet. The doctor wants to make sure everything is healed and working before he goes home (me, too). We are still waiting for his bowels to start working. They go to "sleep" after a surgery. As soon as they start working, he will be able to drink full liquids and then start introducing food. I think he has forgotten what food is after a month in the hospital.

He loves to hear from you. Mail time is one of our favorite times of the day. He is now in his sixth

room in the hospital. The nurses requested that he
be moved back up the seventh floor. I don't know if it
is because he is such a good patient or that he has a
cute butt (did I say that?).

Thanks for all the prayers. We are doing great!

In God's name,
TBEMC

*They were five minutes late. The doctors were supposed to
come get him for his procedure five minutes ago. I couldn't say
anything because that would be insensitive, but I was starving.
Mom and I always went to Bruegger's Bagels on the other side
of campus at the U of M when Dad went into his procedures, but
Mom told me we couldn't talk about it in front of him because he
couldn't eat beforehand, and he had to be awake during the entire
procedure in case they hit a major nerve. But still, I was starving.*

*"They'll be here any minute," Dad said, proving I wasn't
doing a good job at hiding my impatience, "and then you can
go explore campus and get your breakfast." He didn't look up
from the magazine he was flipping through, but he was smiling.*

*We were sitting in a waiting room for patients, which was
unlike the other waiting rooms we were usually in. It wasn't
comfortable or cozy; the floor was a dirty once-white tile, and
the fluorescent lights overhead were bright and buzzed in the
quiet of the room. There was a stale smell that hung in the air,
and instead of a door, there was just an opening in the wall, so
we were sitting and facing the check-in counter. We had been
in this room a few times, but only for procedures like this one.
This was where we sat when we waited with Dad, but there was
a larger, more comfortable waiting room for us to go to once
they took him.*

Like clockwork, two men in green scrubs with blue masks around their necks came around the corner. "Tom," one of them said impersonally to the small waiting room, scanning the faces of the men in the room to see who was alerted by the sound of his name. Mom stood up with Dad and gave him a kiss before he walked away to join them.

"Finally," I said once they were out of sight, and she laughed.

We stepped out of the building and turned left on the sidewalk, making our way towards the part of campus where the strip of restaurants was located. "We have about three hours to burn," she said. "We need to be back before they are done, so Dad doesn't have to wait for us." I nodded. That seemed fair.

As we walked, there were students of the university walking in every direction. They all had headphones over their ears and backpacks on their backs. Every once and a while, we'd see a group of doctors walking together, or I assumed they were doctors because of their white coats over their shirts and ties. It was the springtime, so there were puddles of melted snow in the dips in the sidewalks, and it was warm enough outside for a sweatshirt or a light jacket.

"The party's at Sally's," Mom whispered to me as we walked.

"What? What are you talking about? Who's Sally?"

She smiled and repeated herself, again whispering, "The party's at Sally's."

I looked up and saw a sign with a squirrel in a pink cheerleading costume in front of what appeared to be a bar called Sally's, and underneath the name it read, "The party's at Sally's." Why Mom needed to whisper this to me, I had no idea, but it was funny. I laughed and looked ahead to see how far our bagel shop was from Sally's — it was just down the street.

We ordered our usual: two bagels and a small tub of cream cheese. We liked to order the tubs so we could bring back any extra for bagels at home. There was something about the warm and toasted bagels with the flavored cream cheeses that we loved. Everyone around here viewed this place as just another fast food or breakfast place, but we loved it.

When we finished our breakfast, we ventured back outside and headed towards the bridge that crossed over the Mississippi River. It was a huge double-layer bridge; the top was for pedestrians and people on bikes, and the bottom was for cars. In the middle of the top bridge was a covered section to protect walkers from the wind in the winter. It wasn't heated, but I'm sure the covering helped if this was anyone's daily commute to work or school.

"Come here. Look over the edge with me." Mom was on her tiptoes, leaning into the wall on the edge of the bridge, looking down at the river rushing below us. I didn't have a fear of heights, but this still made my knees shake a little.

"I don't like graffiti," Mom said, now pointing at the side of a tall cement wall that contained the river, "but that's impressive." She was right. She was pointing at beautiful artwork of a clearly talented graffiti artist, but it was on a place that was seemingly unreachable.

We both stood on the bridge, leaning into the wall and looking around us in every direction for several minutes. We looked at the water, the buildings and factories on the other side of the river, the buildings of campus that we could see from where we stood, and the blue sky above us, which was unfamiliar after the long winter we had just faced.

"Let's go back," I said. "I know we still have some time, but I should work on some homework before Dad is done."

"Good idea. I brought along some puzzle books."

A few hours later, as I was tackling some math worksheets, one of the men in the green scrubs from that morning was in the doorway of the waiting room and looking at us. "Tom's family?"

"That's us," Mom answered.

"Will you come with me, please? We're all done, and we'd like to meet with you to talk about some of the coverage Dr. Fisher was able to get today."

Mom started to ask the man some questions, but he explained that she needed to wait to ask Dr. Fisher because it was his procedure and his place to explain results. We followed him into the elevator, down several floors, and then down a long hallway with the same dirty white tile floors and fluorescent lights as in the waiting room from that morning.

We approached a tall, skinny man with blue scrubs, a blue mask around his neck that I assumed was recently over his mouth and nose, and thick caterpillar-like eyebrows above the frames of his glasses: Dr. Fisher. I remembered him from previous appointments. There was a time when we were in a small conference room in a clinic waiting to meet with him. Dad had gone to the bathroom, so Mom and I did our puzzle books. She had a crossword book, and I had a brain teasers workbook. Dr. Fisher had arrived before Dad came back, so he sat next to me and helped me solve some of the brain teasers I was working on. He was introducing himself and telling us that he cross-country skied to work in the winters and jogged to work in the summers. The look on Dad's face when he came back to the conference room was a hilarious look of surprise. I imagined that seeing your daughter work on brain teasers and talk about cross-country skiing with the doctor who will attempt to cure you of cancer is quite the sight to see.

This time, though, Dr. Fisher's face was not friendly, animated, or full of expression as it had been on that day. Where he stood, there were a few nurses behind him, and Dad was sitting in a wheelchair in front of him with his back to us.

"Good. You're here," Dr. Fisher said. "I'm sorry we're in a hallway. We're surrounded by operating rooms, not meeting rooms, and they're all being used by other patients. I have some

sensitive information to share with you all, and I didn't want to wait until we had a more traditional place to meet. I hope this will work."

"It's fine," Mom answered. Her eyes were full of worry and fear. Considering all that was probably happening behind each door of this long hallway, it was surprisingly quiet where we stood. I looked at Dad's back and wondered if he was in any pain as he sat there. He wasn't speaking, and he hadn't turned around to greet us. He was usually groggy and tired after these procedures, but he wasn't in a bed, so I figured he couldn't be sleeping, especially since the doctor was meeting with us.

Before Dr. Fisher continued talking, he shot me a quick look. His facial expression was questioning if I should be here for this, or if I should be somewhere else so my parents could explain what he was about to share in a way that was better suited for a young girl my age to hear. But his look didn't linger, and he never mentioned my presence. He could likely tell I wasn't there by accident.

"I want to start off by telling you that we got some great coverage today. We were able to see more of the pelvic area than we have been able to see thus far." His eyes were serious, and he let his focus bounce between Mom and Dad, and he never looked at me again. "However, in order to do that, we needed to go through a major nerve in the thigh of his right leg." Mom and Dad were motionless. Dr. Fisher had their complete attention.

"I'm optimistic about where we can go from here, now that we know what we are dealing with," he said. "But there is a downside to this." Now he was only looking at Dad. "There is some irreversible damage to the nerve in your thigh. With some physical therapy and the use of a cane, it will be functional, but, to put it bluntly, you will never be able to walk normally or run again."

Dr. Fisher didn't break his eye contact with Dad; he hardly even blinked. No one said anything for quite a while, and I let my focus bounce back and forth between Dr. Fisher's and Mom's faces. She did not move or speak, but I saw that her eyes were forming tears that were beginning to stream down her face. I looked at Dad again, and he was not saying anything, and he had still not turned around, so I couldn't see his face. Mom, crying, took a step forward and put her hand on his left shoulder, and he put one hand on hers and another over his eyes while his shoulders began to shake.

CHAPTER 8

"HI. FOR THOSE OF YOU who don't know me, I'm Dave Wiechmann." When I looked at Dave standing up in front of all these people, all I could imagine was his crooked smile and how he dug up my backyard to plant that tree. "I'm a long, longtime friend of Tom and Becky's," he said. "When most people talk about Tom and the fun times they've had, cards come up a lot of the time. But I believe that the most important things you want to remember about somebody are not just the fun times, but what you've learned from them.

"So, my memory of Tom goes back a long way. Probably about two decades ago, Tom and I were playing cards against Becky and Beth in Huron, South Dakota. We were playing Whist; Tom and I were up 12-0. Of course, I was getting very cocky and letting my mouth go off about how we were beating them, probably saying some sexist remarks about how women can't play cards. Tom tried to stop me, telling me that anything could happen. What he was basically telling me was, 'Win like a man with some grace and style.' Of course, Becky and Beth came back to kick our butts." He paused to let the congregation laugh at his story.

"But the lesson remains," he continued. "This is how Tom really led his life, with grace and respect for every moment. There are some people who live with regrets, what they should have done or what they should have said. One of the last times Tom and I got to talk to each other, just one-on-one, without a bunch of people standing around asking whose deal it was, we talked about his cancer. We discussed his treatments and everything he had gone through over the years. There was no regret in his voice at all. He said that with everything that had passed, everything that he went through was worth it, and he would do it every step of the way again. The time that he was able to spend with his family, with Becky and the girls, was more important than anything else he faced." Dave looked around the sanctuary and spoke as if my dad might be standing out there watching him speak. "Tom led his life with the cards that life dealt him. He did it with grace, courage, and no regrets." When he finished, he looked up from his paper and stared at my mom. He just looked at her before shooting a half-smile at her and then looking down and walking back to his seat.

Andrew Thostenson, Gayle's husband, was next to speak. Andrew was about 6'6", loud, and a genius. He was known at our church as the "computer guy" who knew how to fix any computer-related problem.

"How many people know what a statistician is?" Andrew began. He paused and took a deep breath. "Bean counter, number cruncher, mathematics nutcase." He continued to recount memories of my dad and how he knew him on more of a professional level, rather than personal.

When he finished, Dwight and Lisa Steffen, my parents' best friends and my second parents, made their way up to the podium. Lisa grabbed the microphone and stood there, eyes filling up with tears, not saying a word. Dwight stood to her left with a blank expression on his face.

Through her tears, Lisa finally let out the shaky words, "I'm Lisa Steffen." She paused again, doing her best to regain the strength that those three words had cost her. "I know Tom and Becky through church." Tears began to run down her cheeks, but she pushed through and said what she wanted to say.

"After the services, Tom and Dwight would sit downstairs and talk their farm talk, which did not really impress us women. When they moved here, we realized that they only lived a block away from us." She continued talking about how she and my mom quickly became close friends, along with Dwight and my dad, and that they worked together for programs in the church.

"The door to their house was always open," she said. "Being her best friend, I took up a lot of Becky's time. After a while, she gave me the code to their garage. I'm not sure how Tom felt about that, allowing me to come over whenever I pleased, but I'm sure he loved it." The congregation laughed as she shared her memories.

"Tom was a very, very loving man. Whenever you had a problem, he knew how to calm you down, offer you some perspective, and help you figure it out. He helped me to be calm and not all worked up, as I normally would be. He was just an all-around great guy. Tom, thank you for giving me Becky because —" she was cut off by her emotions getting the best of her. She, again, fought through her tears with a shaky voice. "I could not do anything in this world without her. Thank you." She began to cry harder, so she handed the microphone to Dwight. With his arm around Lisa, he looked at the microphone, readying himself to speak. He looked up at the crowd of people as his eyes filled with tears. Dwight focused his attention on my mom, said a quiet, "I'm sorry," put the microphone down, and led Lisa back to their seats.

There was a long silence as the congregation sat in their seats and cried. It is astounding to me that one person can affect so many people in such a deep and passionate way. The loss of one man caused an entire church filled with people to sit together and simply cry.

After a few seconds, my mom stood and made her way to the front of the sanctuary. I had no idea she had prepared anything to say, and after seeing her the past few days, I didn't know if she could make it through an entire speech.

"I'm not sure how I can follow that one," she began. She took a deep breath. "I don't know how many times people have asked us, 'How do you do it? How can you be so strong?' Our responses were that we were never given a choice. Tom and I would have never chosen to have cancer for seven years. What I would like to tell you about were the choices that we *were* allowed to make. I did choose to go out on a blind date with my friend's boyfriend's cousin. Tom did choose to go on a blind date with his cousin's girlfriend's friend." The congregation let out a laugh between tears.

"From that moment on, we made our choices together. We chose to move to Colorado and spend four years getting to know each other and depending on each other as a couple. We started our lives together camping in the Rockies, exploring Colorado Springs, watching movies on HBO, loving two kittens, lying on the couch together, starting our careers, and loving each other.

"We chose to move closer to home to start our family. We had Emma when we lived in Brookings, South Dakota. We had Mary when we lived in Lafayette, Indiana. We had Claire when we lived in West Fargo, North Dakota. And we chose to stop moving." She paused again as people laughed. "We were fulfilled by being parents and watching our creations grow and become beautiful, talented, spirited, and unique ladies.

"We chose to follow God. As each day of our lives passed, we grew stronger in our love and dependence on Him." Her voice trembled and shook as she forced her way through, despite the emotions that were unwilling to subside. "We realized that all of our choices were not ours alone. We did not choose cancer. What cancer did for us was make us appreciate the choices that we did make. We chose God, we chose family, and we chose the love of friends. If I had to do it all over again, knowing what I know now, I again would choose Tom DeJong. Thank you."

She quickly put down the microphone and walked back to her seat. Before she made it to her spot in the pew, Beth stood up to hug her. My mom stood there and let Beth wrap her arms around her, supporting and comforting her. I just watched them, thinking of how incredibly brave my mom was.

There was a long break when no one moved or said anything. Eventually, Carol Sterup, one of my Dad's good friends from the church, slowly walked to the front. "I have some things to say, but I don't know if I can talk and then sing for you, so I'll get myself on the right note and go from there," she said. Without any music to accompany her, she began to sing. I thought of my dad and his cancer, and how he had once told me that he felt like whenever she sang, she was singing to him. The two of them shared a bond I would never understand, but it was something that deeply touched both of them.

She stopped singing in the middle of the song, and as the tears flowed down her cheeks, she focused her attention on my mom. Crying, she continued her song. "We find the strength to press on, Lord, to press on," she sang. She clicked off the microphone and quickly walked to her seat near the back of the sanctuary.

Matt walked up to the podium to conclude the service. "Let us pray."

DECEMBER 4, 2005

Sometimes all you can do is laugh.

He is not home yet, but I think we are getting closer.

Thanksgiving was great. I can't remember the last time that I had three days where all I had to worry about was getting home for a shower. The girls had a fun Thanksgiving in South Dakota with their grandparents and made it back to North Dakota before the storm hit. They had two snow days. They were thrilled, and I got my Christmas decorations up. Oh yes, this is supposed to be about Tom.

Tuesday was our nineteenth wedding anniversary. The girls made us a wonderful video of past pictures. We loved it.

On Wednesday, Tom had his catheter removed. This procedure went fine. On Thursday, during a dressing change, the nurse found a new lump to the right of his tailbone. He had a CT scan done in the afternoon. What it wasn't was the bowel leaking or an infection. It is probably the cancer growing. Chemo will be a discussion, but not for a while.

When the approval finally came for Tom to come home, I had already gone home. He called me and was singing "I'll Be Home for Christmas" to me on the phone. I asked him to sing again, but he said no. I guess you have to take what you can get!

Here's the part you have to shake your head at. On Saturday morning, he started running a fever of 100, so now they are keeping him for observation to see what is causing the fever. I guess what would have been worse is if I had taken him home and then had to take him right back to the hospital. I did think we had made it. Now we wait from day to day.

I am hoping that the next email that I write will be after he is home, and who knows? Maybe he will be writing it.

Merry Christmas and God bless,
TBEMC

DECEMBER 23, 2005

Tom is home! Merry Christmas!

All good news to report. My mother came from Arkansas to stay with us for a while to help out. She has been a true blessing. We also had a home health nurse and a physical therapist come out for several visits to make sure that we were on the right track.

We had our follow-up doctor's appointments this past week. Tom has been released from his infectious disease doctor. Tom's surgeon wants us to keep in contact, but we have no scheduled appointments. Tom's oncologist wants him to start chemo in January. (We knew this would happen, but we put it off until after the holidays.)

After two months of paperwork and many people working for us, we finally got Tom's motorized wheelchair. It is very nice. It gives him so much freedom and independence when we are out and about. It is very heavy, and we need a ramp to get it out of the house and into the van. We have many friends who are our angels, and who joined together and got a ramp for us. Thank you doesn't seem like enough to say, so hopefully they know that it means so much more to us than words can say.

We have gotten Tom out of the house for several events: church, Mary's basketball, an office party, and most importantly, Christmas shopping. Tom is gaining strength every day, and his spirits continue to inspire all of us. We feel blessed to be able to be together this Christmas season, and we won't take a moment of it for granted. Please treasure your time spent with your family and loved ones.

May Jesus and God be with you,
TBEMC

CHAPTER 9

THE NEXT MORNING, WE ARRIVED at the church about half an hour before the funeral service began. People were filing into the sanctuary, as well as the basement in the Fellowship Hall where a projector was set up—there were more people than seats upstairs. My family was huddled together in one of the Sunday School rooms in the basement, readying ourselves to walk into the sanctuary together.

It was raining outside, a fairly heavy rainfall. From the basement, we could hear the raindrops pelting against the windows of the building and thunder sounding outside. Matt came downstairs to the room where we stood, dressed in his black Sunday robe, and asked us if we were ready to begin.

We followed him up the stairs but stopped before we reached the top. "It's already a little after 10:00, but people keep walking in," Matt said, clearly flustered about delaying the service.

We stood on the stairs for a few minutes longer. I stood next to Emma and Claire, who I would be sitting next to upstairs, just as I had the night before.

After about five more minutes had passed, a blinding light shone through the church windows as lightning struck the ground outside. Almost immediately, an incredible echoing boom shook the building.

"I think Tom says it's time to start," my mom said to Matt in the front of the group. We all let out a little laugh as we straightened ourselves up and filed into the sanctuary.

I had never seen the sanctuary so full of people. There were multiple rows of people standing behind the pews, not including the people downstairs. As we made our way to the front rows, my eye caught Rich, Jake, and Jamison sitting together along the aisle. Jake and Jamison had on plaid button-down shirts and had their hair combed down, a change from their usual scraggly look.

A few rows up from them sat an entire row filled with my closest friends. I saw the backs of Katelyn, Andrea, and Danielle sitting next to each other along the aisle, and I grabbed Andrea's shoulder as I walked by. As I passed, I turned to look at them, only to see each of their eyes already filled with tears.

"Christ has been raised from the dead," Matt began. "For since death came through a human being, the resurrection of the dead has also come through a human being. For as all die in Adam, so all will be made alive in Christ." He welcomed everyone to the church in remembrance and celebration of my dad's life, and then led us all in prayer.

Claire and four other girls from our church walked up to the front of the sanctuary to perform a dance to the song "Awesome God." The performance included both dance choreography as well as sign language with the lyrics. The five girls held straight faces throughout the entire dance. I looked down the pew to see my mom and Beth, both watching impassively, but with a steady stream of tears running down their cheeks. My dad's parents were directly to my right, and both held hard and emotionless faces throughout the whole performance.

"All have sinned and fall short of the glory of God," Matt continued. He then led the congregation in reading aloud the prayer of confession, followed by Matt explaining how we all have been forgiven for our sins. He continued by reading scripture from the Bible, along with explanations of each verse.

As we stood to sing "On Eagle's Wings," I looked around at everyone singing. I turned to see my dad's aunts and uncles standing a few rows behind us. The men all had serious expressions, and the women were all crying. I looked up at my grandparents next to me to see them both crying. My grandma caught my eye and put her arm around me. My grandpa did not sing, but just stared forward as he let his tears run from his red, swollen eyes.

After the song was finished, Matt began to recount his own personal stories of knowing my dad. "It is a small and strange world sometimes," he began. "I'll bet many of you don't know that I met Tom before either of us ever moved to West Fargo. See, we played against each other in a church softball league back in my hometown of West Lafayette, Indiana many years ago. Tom and I didn't know each other well at that time, but imagine our surprise when we discovered this connection, years later, in the first days after I came to this church. I remember distinctly that Tom was one of the very first people here with whom I sat down and had a really good sports conversation. And that's something that meant a great deal to me, as I tried to get my feet under me in a new job, a new community, really, a whole new world.

"Love of sports, young families, a history in Indiana, this church: Tom and I definitely had some things in common. I think that maybe these connections are part of why I can't help but be deeply affected by his death, as I know all of you are as well.

"I can't help but reflect a little on the awfulness, the seeming unfairness of it all. I mean, why should Tom have to go through such a thing? Why should Becky and the girls be left without him? It just doesn't make sense. It doesn't seem right. And what's more, we have met here today, and I'm offering these reflections in a place where over and over, week in and week out, we affirm that the will of God is sovereign, that it is powerful and effective in shaping the world. So does that mean that this awful thing that has happened to Tom was God's will? That question is what haunts me. I mean, how could God will such a thing for his dear children?"

When Matt preached every Sunday, I always did my best to pay close attention to everything he said, to let every word sink in. Yet, no matter how hard I tried, my mind always fell in and out between focusing on his sermons and wandering around the room. This morning, though, he had my complete attention.

"But on the other hand," he continued, "if He didn't, how could it have happened at all? As always, when we go looking for answers about God and His ways with the world, we must turn first to the scriptures, wherein He reveals Himself to us."

Matt went on to explain how God protects his children and that He is always working for our good. "The God we know from the Bible would not, I believe, wish any of His precious children to suffer as Tom did," he continued. "Even if, as Tom and his family have done and continue to do, they bore up under this burden with exemplary courage and grace and good cheer." He paused and scanned the faces of all of us in the front row to emphasize that he was speaking directly to us. "I will be so bold today as to say that the disease that has assailed Tom for so long, and that finally overcame his body this past week, was *not* the will of God. Instead, Tom's cancer, like all the suffering and illness and pain and grief that has been a part of the experience of humanity since the days of Adam, that cancer was a consequence of the corruption of God's good creation by generation after generation after generation of human sinfulness and error."

I had never before considered any of the things that he was saying. I knew that not even a blade of grass moved without God knowing, but I had never thought about whether or not

He wanted it to move. I had just assumed that whenever bad things happened, it was so we would appreciate the good. What Matt was saying, about my dad's death not being God's will, was slightly overwhelming to me.

"God forgives our sins, but they still have consequences," Matt said. "And after so very long, our sins and all the sins of all the world have made this world a place where terrible things sometimes happen. This is one reason that we confess our sins together when we meet in worship. It's because our guilt and its consequences are a corporate thing, affecting all the world, not just ourselves as individuals. In His wisdom, from the very beginning, God granted us freedom: freedom of thought, freedom of will, freedom of action. We are here today as witnesses to one of the sad things that the world has done with this freedom." Matt looked around at the desolate faces staring back at him. His eyebrows furrowed as he matter-of-factly told us something that, at that moment, I knew I would never forget: "God never willed that Tom or anyone else suffer and die in the prime of life."

He took a second to let what he had just said sink in, and then he let his words pick up speed as he continued. "But if Tom's disease was not the will of God, if it was, as I have claimed, contrary to what God wills, then where was this powerful and active God of whom I've been speaking through all of this experience? Where can we see the will of God at work in what has gone on here? Look again, I would suggest, at Psalm 81. Here, God speaks to his people saying, 'I relieve your shoulder of the burden. Your hands were freed from the basket. In distress you called, and I rescued you.'" He stopped and looked up. He put his hands on the sides of the podium and let his weight lean onto his arms. Slowly, he began to speak. "It *was* the will of God that Tom finally be relieved of the burden that had laid him low, that he be freed from the shackles of weakness and pain by which the cancer tried and failed to conquer his spirit." Again, he paused and looked directly at my mom in the first pew. "It is by nothing else but the will of God that Tom has been called home to see his heavenly Father in person, and to be redeemed from all that afflicted him here on Earth," he said.

He put his hands into the air and spoke directly to the crowd in front of him. "Friends, by the will of God, and by the all-sufficient grace of Jesus Christ, Tom has traded in his mortal life for an eternal membership in the Church Triumphant, a place in the congregation of the saints in glory. He is a forerunner, if you will, one of the first fruits of a great harvest that will one day include us all. Tom has passed from the pain of the here and now to the boundless joy of the eternal, becoming the person that God made him to be, full of grace and truth and joy and wonder.

"So, if you must grieve this day, if you must weep for the loss that we all feel, do so. And do so without shame, knowing that your tears and your grief honor Tom and his memory. But because Tom is a beloved child of God, temper your grief with rejoicing. Rejoice in the victory over cancer and weakness and pain that Tom has been given and that will last for all time. And thinking on this victory, thinking on the mercy and the grace of God, we can say with confidence, His will be done. Amen."

Matt folded up his papers and turned to head back to his seat to the left of the podium, as Carol Sterup once again made her way up to the front to sing to Dad. I still held my composure; I sat up straight and kept my tears back. But I knew that I was one of only a few in the sanctuary who could truthfully say this.

Listening to Carol sing, I was brought back to a Sunday about two years ago, after my mom and sisters had already gone home after church, and I had decided to stay back with my dad. He was talking to Carol in the Fellowship Hall long after the rest of the congregation had already filed out, family by family. Letting the two of them talk alone, I had gone upstairs to sit on the bench by the front door. When Dad finally limped up the stairs with his cane, he had a solemn expression on his face. Without a word, I stood up to walk with him, and together we made our way down the long sidewalk toward his Jeep in the parking lot.

As we walked, I put my head down and watched his red cane take the place of his right leg as he took each step. Rarely was Dad ever silent like this, so I figured I should just let him be.

"We're going to get through this," he finally said.

"What do you mean?" I asked him.

"We're going to beat this cancer."

"How you know?"

He stopped walking and looked at me. "Because Carol said we would."

Claire was tapping my knee, bringing my attention back to the funeral. "Look," she whispered. She looked back to her right and pointed at the pew filled with my friends. Every girl in that row was sobbing; they were past crying. I looked at them with a concerned look on my face. One by one they each looked at me, tried to contain their tears, and did their best to force themselves to smile at me.

As Carol finished her song, Matt slowly walked back up to the podium to lead us in prayer.

To conclude the service, Claire proudly and confidently walked up to the front of the sanctuary to begin the closing hymn, "Amazing Grace," on her recorder. She furrowed her eyebrows and concentrated on her fingers in front of her. With no accompanying instrument or voices, the single sound of her recorder played throughout the room with a slowness and a sadness that was felt by everyone who listened. At the start of the second verse, the organist began to play, and we knew that was our cue to join in. The sounds of the congregation's voices were quiet and trembling, as the words were forced through grief and heartache.

JANUARY 19, 2006

Well, it finally happened. It was a day we had been hoping for for a long time. Tom went back to work! He was understandably nervous and excited at the same time. He was greeted with a "welcome back" banner, and the fact that the office had made accommodations for his wheelchair was fantastic. When he got back to his desk, he saw piles of work waiting for him. This could have been overwhelming, but for Tom, I saw a sparkle return to his eyes and a look of anticipation to get started. He told me I could go and come back later.

I thought it seemed interesting that Tom was admitted to the hospital on the eighteenth of October, and three months later on the eighteenth of January, he went back to work. I know that I will have to slow him down and not let him overdo it. When I went back to pick him up, he was on his way to a teleconference and was talking about a trip to Minot next week. I surprised him by not saying no.

On the medical side, all tubes were removed last Monday. There is still a small leak in the bowel, but the doctors say that his body will re-absorb the extra urine and that urine is sterile and won't hurt him. He also started chemo last Monday. He will go in weekly for infusions but will only receive the chemo every three weeks.

Thanks for the continued prayers. I am greatly enjoying reporting good news.

In God's name,
TBEMC

JUNE 14, 2006

I know that I haven't written for a while, and
everyone has been asking how Tom is doing. We had a
plan that we were going to follow this summer, but
somehow cancer doesn't like to follow our plans. In
May, Tom had his last chemo treatment. We had decided
that he would take off June and July from chemo so
that he could enjoy the summer. He had a CAT scan at
the end of May, and those results were going to help
us decide what to do after July. The results did show
progression of the cancer in the lungs. We weren't too
surprised; although, naturally, disappointed.

What did happen about four weeks ago was that Tom
and I both got colds. My cold got better after about
three days, but his kept getting worse, especially the
cough. We were worried about pneumonia and even took
him to the emergency room one night. For once, the
doctors didn't tell us the worst answer. He had a sinus
infection and a bladder infection. He was put on two
different antibiotics, so I thought that once those
had run their course, he would start feeling better.
He didn't, and still hasn't started feeling better.

Because of his prolonged stay in bed and a lack
of eating and a combination of many other things, he
has become very weak. At this point, he has trouble
standing because of the pain in his hip, and his legs
are so weak that they barely support him. Yesterday
was the first day in weeks that he has shown an interest
in strengthening his legs, so we are having a physical
therapist come to the house this morning.

Emma, Mary, and I had a family reunion in Ohio that we went to last week. We had a good time, but we were very nervous about leaving Tom. We were fortunate that Tom's dad was able to come and stay with him. I think that they were able to spend some very valuable time together. At this point, Tom gets tired very easily, but we do have a ramp and an electric wheelchair that allow him to get out to take walks around the block and watch the girls play in the yard. We will be sticking pretty close to home this summer, but we have plenty of room in the house for any visitors who find their way up north.

Have a great and relaxing summer,
TBEMC

CHAPTER 10

AT THE CONCLUSION OF "AMAZING Grace," I knew it was time to stand up and face everyone who had come to mourn with us. As I neared the aisle and began to make my way to the back of the church, I looked at all the faces staring back at me, tears filling their eyes. I could feel my own tears forming, but I didn't want them to come out. I didn't want anyone to see.

I approached the pew filled with my best friends, from school and from basketball, and they all wiped their eyes and gave me the best smiles they could muster. I looked behind them to a pew filled with their parents. My eyes scanned, person to person, until it reached the end of the row. Jon Holland, Katelyn's dad and my traveling basketball coach, was staring right into my eyes, his filled with tears. This was more than I could handle, and I felt my lips begin to quiver. I blinked hard as I looked away, and the tears began to stream down my cheeks.

For the rest of the way through the sanctuary of the church, I looked down at my feet and cried as I walked. I couldn't quite figure out why I was crying. I'd had more than enough time to prepare for this. I knew it was coming, and I knew I would miss him, but it seemed a little dramatic to cry over it. And besides, I already did. I cried the night he died. Wasn't that enough?

Outside of the sanctuary, my sisters and I followed my mom to the church basement where we took an immediate turn into one of the Sunday School classrooms, closed the door, and sat down on the couches to regroup.

We looked at each other and, without saying anything, we knew we needed to try our best to compose ourselves. The church was filled with people who would all want to talk to us. Mom and Emma were crying, but Claire just sat there, uncomfortable and nervous.

"Are my eyes all red and puffy?" I asked.

"Shut up, Mary," Emma muttered. "No one cares." She turned away and wiped her own eyes.

My mom looked at me. "No, your eyes look fine."

There was a knock on the door, and Lisa popped her head inside. She was holding a box of Kleenex and some lemonade. "How are you girls holding up?"

My mom smiled and walked over to hug her. "Thank you," she said.

When we finally made an appearance downstairs in the Fellowship Hall of the church, I walked straight to my friends' table.

"Hey, Mar," Danielle said.

"Hey, guys."

"That was really nice," Katelyn added, and I nodded.

I looked across the room at my mom clutching one of the many hand-held fans that were floating around. The air conditioning in the church was broken, so when it got hot outside, it was miserable inside, and the fans helped. A little.

"Here, how is this?" Grandma Fidler said to Megan, one of my friends sitting at the table. She had noticed that Megan had been fanning herself with her hand, so she held up her hair to cool the back of her neck with one of the little battery-powered fans.

"Oh, thank you," Megan said as she let her shoulders drop and allowed herself to sink deeper into her chair.

I walked towards my grandparents, who were sitting with the DeJong side of my family and some high school friends of my dad's.

"Hey there, Mary," my grandpa said as he reached out to grab my hand. He pulled me onto his knee. I used to think this was a thing grandpas did with their little grandchildren, but as I grew older, he still always did this. I'll probably be twenty years old, and Grandpa will still pull me to sit on his knee.

"Hi, Grandpa."

"How are you, hun?" my grandma asked me.

"I'm hot."

She smiled at me. "I think we all are."

Some of Dad's friends were at the end of the table discussing farming and were comparing stories from their own experiences. Having never been around farming, I didn't really understand the language, but I still liked listening to it. I knew that if Dad was here, this was the table he would be sitting at, and he would have been right in the middle, adding his two cents whenever the opportunity came.

"Oh, no!" Grandma Fidler yelled from across the room. I whipped my head around to look.

"Ouch, ouch, ouch!" Megan screamed, holding her hair.

"I'm so sorry! I don't know how this happened!" Apparently, my grandma's fan had gotten too close to Megan's hair and was now all tangled in it.

By the time I reached the table, my grandma, Lisa, and my mom were behind Megan, trying to free her from the fan. I looked at her and laughed. "Your face is so red." She glared back at me.

"Mary, be nice," my mom said without looking up from the mess of hair.

"Well," I said, defending myself, "it is."

"Do I get a hug before I leave?" I turned around to see my sixth-grade teacher, Mrs. Ryan, smiling at me with open arms. Without saying anything, I took a step closer and let her wrap me in a hug. "I'm so, so sorry, Mary. I can't even imagine what you're feeling right now."

I looked up at her and smiled. "Thank you. I'm doing okay, though."

Keeping her hands on my shoulders, she took a step back, fully extending her arms. She seemed as if she was trying to stop herself from crying, and just when I thought she might say something, she blinked away tears, and merely smiled at me before walking away.

JUNE 21, 2006

Two nights ago, Mary and I took Tom to the hospital. There were many factors, but the most urgent ones seemed to be the fact that he had stopped eating for a day and a half, he was having headaches, he was having trouble remembering things, he wasn't able to stand or transfer safely to and from his wheelchair, and he was throwing up immediately after eating, which meant that none of his pain medication was getting in his system.

I suppose any of these reasons alone would be sufficient to take him in, but in combination, we definitely had no choice. When we got to the hospital they put him on fluids and gave him two doses of pain medication to make him comfortable. They also did a CT scan of his brain and found that part of his cerebellum was abnormal. They weren't sure if this was caused by a stroke or if the cancer had gone to his brain.

They tried to take Tom in for an MRI, but things didn't go well because he was not able to lie straight and still for the length of time needed for the MRI. He was brought back to the room and heavily sedated before returning for the second MRI. When I saw him later, he was not aware of anything that was going on. I spent the night at the hospital, and by the morning, I was starting to see Tom again. He was much more responsive and also a little annoyed that he hadn't been told what was going on (he had been). I feel that a little anger is good because that means he is caring about what is happening.

The MRI showed that there were four cancerous lesions on the brain and some swelling within the brain. They immediately started him on Decadron. This is a steroid that helps to reduce the swelling and fluids in the brain. By the morning, he had eaten two good meals, had a good night's sleep, his pain was under control, and the swelling in his brain was reduced. Now what do we do? Barb and Milo, Tom's two brothers and their families, my sister, and the girls were all around. We are all in agreement that we want to give Tom quality of life. If quantity is a bonus, then that is wonderful.

We met with a neurosurgeon, and he will put a shunt into Tom's brain tomorrow morning. This will drain fluid from the brain and relieve pressure. The surgery is only supposed to last for an hour, and under most circumstances, the patient goes home the next day. We are also considering doing radiation on the cancer in the brain. All doctors involved feel that this will improve his mental abilities and could help with his motor abilities. It will not make him sick. My concern is transportation. He may need to stay in the hospital for the treatments, or we may need to find a service that can help get him to and from the hospital.

The girls are strong and worried and continue on with their busy lives. Emma just finished her behind-the-wheel driving course and is playing as much volleyball as she can. Mary is in many different basketball camps and had a big picnic at our house last night with all of her friends and their families. Claire is in soccer and going to start theater in a couple of weeks. I try to keep us all normal and include Tom in as many of our activities as possible. He did go to the movies several times last week, work once, and to Mary's basketball awards.

Claire and I were in church on Sunday, and she said she was going to pray for a miracle. I told her we have already gotten our miracle — seven years of treasuring every moment that we have spent as a family.

Right now I feel comfortable that Tom is being well taken care of, he is safe, and his parents and brothers are coming. Tom's life (and ours) is changing daily. We are along for God's bumpy ride.

We love you all. Thank you for the support and, most importantly, the prayers.

TBEMC

CHAPTER 11

THE HOUSE SEEMED UNUSUALLY CLUTTERED when we returned home from the funeral. There were clothes, food, picture frames, photo albums, and Dad memorabilia hanging all over the house in places where they clearly didn't belong. Mom walked into the house and sighed at the mess. We knew we'd eventually have to clean it all up, but we didn't have enough energy quite yet.

The next morning, I came out of my bedroom and looked into my parents' empty, made bed. I had grown so used to hearing the morning news playing in their room next to mine that it seemed so strange, almost eerie, to wake up to their silent room. The hospital bed where my dad lay only days before was still in the room, almost serving as a reminder of who used to be there, or who should still be there. I could feel my eyes begin to water, so I quickly turned around and headed toward the living room before I lost control of my emotions. I hadn't even had breakfast yet.

"Another country heard from!" my grandma shouted when she spotted me emerging from the hallway. That's Grandma's version of "good morning."

I shot her a sleepy smile. "Morning, Grandma."

"How are you feeling this morning? You hungry for some breakfast?"

I shook my head. "No, thanks. I'm not really hungry. Where's Mom?"

"She went to run some errands before you girls woke up. I told her I could hold down the fort."

"Grandma, you know you don't need to watch us. We can be home alone."

"Give me a break," she said as a guilty smile crept across her face. "I'm at a good place in my book, and it's not easy to read and shop."

I laughed. "And the truth comes out."

Claire came up the stairs, her hair sticking out in every direction. She headed directly to the kitchen to grab the granola bar and chocolate milk that she had every morning.

"Morning," she said groggily.

JULY 1, 2006

For once, Tom was released from the hospital on the day that he was scheduled. In the past, he has gotten fevers or there have been other complications. We have arranged to have hospice help with Tom. They provide a wonderful service, but I am not used to relying on other people for medications and transportation. This will take a little getting used to, but it will be a nice relief. They will send a volunteer to the house to sit with Tom when we want to go to church or if we have other engagements where we all have to be gone.

Tom has had four out of fourteen radiation treatments. I think his color looks better, but he is still confused

most of the time. He can recognize people and answer
questions correctly, but then he will ask to do the
strangest of things. Some of our stories are quite
amusing. I will be curious to see how the rest of the
treatments go and if they help with his confusion.

We have rearranged the house so that there are two
very comfortable recliners in the room with Tom. If
you would like to see him, please feel free to stop
by. You can relax in the recliner, take a nap, or watch
a movie. I might even pop some popcorn if you choose
a movie that I like.

Have a great July 4th,
TBEMC

JULY 6, 2006

Things are very interesting at home. We are moving
through each day moment-by-moment and experience-by-
experience. This past weekend, our house was filled with
eighteen people. Tom was surrounded, although rather
hectically at times, by loving friends and family.
A special friend, Doug Blue, came to visit. He sat
with Tom and shared stories from their past. Tom was
listening and with him for each story. It was nice to
see him smile and remember. I have noticed with other
visits from friends that if they talk about work or
church or their common interest with Tom, then he can
follow along, but if Tom is given choices or asked
questions about anything in the present, he gets very
confused. I find this interesting and puzzling at the
same time.

We have finished six out of fourteen radiation treatments. We will do one more tomorrow and then think things over during the weekend. It takes a lot out of him to make the trip downtown. The radiologist said it was up to me whether we wanted to continue. He wasn't sure if the benefits were outweighing the exhaustion of getting him to the clinic.

I do have one more bit of news to share, but I want it understood that I DO NOT consider this good news! On Sunday, we asked Tom if he wanted to play cards. He surprised us all by saying yes. We quickly cleared off the table, and I still expected him to change his mind, but he didn't. He has trouble with his fine motor skills, so I got him a Velveeta cheese box to hold his cards. We played a game called Oh, Hell. After one round of using the Velveeta box, he opted to hold the cards in his hands instead. I was impressed. He managed not to go set any of the hands and won (slaughtered) all of us. You must understand that no matter what condition Tom is in, I would never let him win. I think you can see why I was not pleased with the outcome of this game.

I love God, I love Tom, I love the girls, and I am letting that love guide us all in the path that we are taking.

God bless,
TBEMC

JULY 13, 2006

Good morning. It is 4:30 in the morning, and I have just given Tom his much-loved glass of water. I tried to go back to sleep but started thinking about the past two weeks. Tom will have been home for two weeks on Friday. When I think of the things that he could do when he got home that he can't do now, I am saddened. This part of the disease doesn't seem fair because it has taken away who Tom is. I am not telling you this to make you sad, but instead, I would like to share the positive things that have happened.

The hospice program is wonderful. It has allowed Tom to be a part of our everyday life. The girls can fix their breakfast and eat it in the room with their father. They can give him sips (sometimes gulps) of any liquid that is cool and refreshing (orange juice is a big favorite). Emma fed him huge portions of cantaloupe and watermelon yesterday, and this morning we are going to try some peaches. The girls do not have to stop their lives and activities to sit in a hospital room. They are active in their sports and social lives and can come home and share that with their dad. He still tells me that he loves me and tells me to have sweet dreams.

We have had healing visits from many friends and family. Tom does know who you are. It is scary and may be easy to stay away, but you will be comforted by seeing Tom. You will know that he is comfortable, well cared-for, loved, and at peace with God.

We are holding tight to God,
TBEMC

"I know it was only about three years ago when we went here, but I feel like it's a school for babies now," Danielle said, staring down the sidewalk towards L.E. Berger, the elementary school that she, Nicole, and I had gone to.

"Stupid Berger," Katelyn said to the three of us with a hint of competitive rivalry. "South Elementary is where it's at."

The four of us decided that now that we were wise and mature going-to-be eighth graders, we might as well vandalize the inside of the biggest blue tubular slide at the elementary school a block away from Danielle's house. However, these particular girls, myself included, were known for being "goodie-goodies," so by vandalizing, we meant that we were going to write something on a piece of paper and tape it to the inside of the slide — a very sturdy tape job, of course.

It was about 8 p.m., and although the sun was beginning to set around us, the summer's heat still held up — a steady eighty-five degrees.

I led our group up to the top of the playground where there was a small platform directly in front of the entrance of the slide, which was just big enough for four girls to sit facing each other.

"What should we write?" Nicole asked us. "It has to be something good, something nobody will understand."

"Our initials!" Danielle yelled excitedly.

"No," Katelyn said nervously looking around. "They'll trace it back to us."

"Okay, first of all," I began, "you didn't even go here. And second, how in the world would they trace three letters of four different people back to us? There's no way."

"Okay, Mary," Danielle said as she began to play mediator. "What if we do our initials to make words? That could be kind of cool."

I popped open the cap of a marker we brought along and positioned the paper on my leg so I could write what I was told.

"Let's see," Danielle thought aloud. "Three names, so three words. Obviously we'll have to start with our middle names."

"Obviously," I said, slightly making fun of what a big deal we were making this almost-vandalism.

"Two Elizabeths," she continued, "Rae, and my middle name is Erin. E, E, E, and R."

"You can't make a word with three vowels and a consonant," I said.

"Yes, I know that," she snapped. "Let's just remember that and move on. All right, our first names will go next. Mary, Nicole, Katelyn, and Danielle."

"No vowels. This isn't going to work," I said as I put the cap back on the marker.

"What if we mix it up?" Katelyn suggested. "And we could use Andrea, too. I know she's not here, but she's still part of our group."

"Yeah, that could work," Danielle agreed. "Then we'd get a few more letters to work with, too. Okay, Mary, start writing."

I rolled my eyes and opened the marker again, looking expectantly at the girls in front of me.

"So, middle names first, right?" Danielle said. "Elizabeth, Elizabeth, Rae, Erin, and Andrea's middle name is Leigh. Isn't it?" I nodded. "Well, we can either do 'Reeel' or 'Leeer'. Which do you guys want?"

"What does 'Leeer' even mean?" Nicole asked.

"Let's just do 'Reeel.' Okay, what's next?" I said as I wrote down the letters of our first word.

We sat at the top of that slide for another half hour or so, working with our names to come up with three secret words to tape inside the slide. Our finished product turned out to be "Reeel Mad Hens," which stood for Rae, Elizabeth, Elizabeth,

Erin, Leigh; Mary, Andrea, Danielle; and Holland, Eisenzimmer, Nelson. We added an "s" on the end for a little extra flair.

Holding her legs, we held Danielle's body down and inside the tube slide, so she was able to place the paper far enough inside that it couldn't be seen from the platform.

"It's on," she yelled up to us from inside the slide. "You can let go now."

Following her lead, we each slid down the slide with our hands on the walls so we would fall slowly enough to see the paper and read the words as we made our way to the bottom.

We could see a storm rolling in from the distance, so we decided we should head back to Danielle's house. The entire walk back, Katelyn and Nicole talked about how nervous they were and how bad they felt about what we had just done, as if it was some sort of crime. Even if it was, it was an easily removable crime.

"There you girls are," Diane, Danielle's mom, said as we made our way into the house. "I wondered if you four were going to make it home alive."

"Hi, Mom," Danielle said.

We made our way down to the basement where Danielle's room was, and we all positioned ourselves into a circle on her bed. Nicole instantly brought up some of our classmates' names and began sharing all of the new gossip she had heard. Danielle and Katelyn listened intently, but my mind had wandered elsewhere.

His eye sockets seemed deeper than ever, if that's even possible. But his eyes weren't sunken in; they now actually seemed to be wider than they always had been. He never blinked much anymore, so he had a buildup around his eyes. His mouth seemed dry, and when he talked, his voice was scratchy. His expression never changed. His body never moved. He lay in that bed as if he had no intention of ever doing anything else again.

"Mary?" I heard one of my friends say after what seemed like hours. I looked up and realized they were all staring at me.

I must have zoned out. "What are you thinking about?"

"Nothing," I quickly said, forcing a smile. "Sorry."

"Mar . . . " Danielle cocked her head downward. "What's going on in your head?"

"Seriously, nothing," I lied. "I'm good."

Katelyn and Nicole smiled at me, and then glanced in each other's direction. Danielle's eyes never left mine. "Shut up. Don't give me that. What are you thinking about?"

I shifted my glance back and forth between each of my friends as I considered letting them inside the thoughts that were racing through my mind.

"You guys know what I'm thinking about," I said to them quietly. "The same thing I'm always thinking about."

"You know, it is a pretty big deal," Katelyn said. "It's okay to think about it and be sad."

I forced a half-smile toward her in appreciation. She must have known how hard that was because she didn't smile back. She just stared at me and waited for me to say something.

"I yelled at him the other day," I told them. I forced my eyes downward to my hands and started to pick at my fingernails as I told them what I was thinking. "I basically told him that he's sick and that he's not doing anything to fix it. I didn't want to be mean, but it scares me. He drinks about four or five pops a day, and he doesn't leave his bed."

"He's weak," Danielle began to say, but then she stopped herself to let me continue.

"I know his legs don't really work anymore and that the pop gives him the energy he desperately needs, but so does walking. So does moving around and getting sunlight and fresh air. There are other ways to make yourself live longer than being lazy and drinking your weight in sugar.

"I know this is kind of weird, and a little depressing, but when I was younger, probably about eight or nine, I used to

pray every night that my dad would live until I graduated high school. I would talk to God like he was sitting right in front of me and I was making some kind of deal with him. I'd say things like, 'God, please let my dad live until I graduate high school, or even college. That way, if I don't live in the house anymore, it won't be so hard when he dies.' Isn't that awful? I was just a little kid, and I was asking God to let my dad live until I'm out of the house." I didn't want to look up at my friends, who were sitting there completely silent, holding onto every word I was saying, so I sat with my head down and continued to pick at my fingernails.

"But I haven't said that prayer in a while," I continued. "For the past month, it's been a little different. I know this sounds bad, and you all know I love my dad, but lately I've been asking God to take him. My dad is already gone; that isn't him in my house anymore." I began to talk faster as my mouth poured out the thoughts that had been racing a million miles an hour through my head for the past few weeks.

"My dad moves, plays basketball with me, and he runs, jokes, eats, smiles, and laughs. I can picture him wearing his red sweatpants running down the street and disappearing around the yellow house at the end of the street, heading out on another run. I would shoot hoops until he would come back, and after he jumped rope to finish his workout, he'd shoot with me. Even since he's been sick, he's been at our basketball games, and he sat underneath the basketball hoop in his wheelchair with a Diet Coke in his hand while I shot free throws. He hit the button to make his wheelchair "beep" at me, so of course I missed my shot. Do you remember that?" I didn't look up or even give them a chance to respond. "But now, it's just his body left. The man in my house has to be fed, babysat, and has a hospice nurse come take care of him every day. He doesn't remember who we are, he doesn't blink, and he doesn't make sense when he talks most

of the time. I don't know if that's bad of me or not, but I've been praying every night that he would die. It's what is best for him, right? I mean, it's clearly going to happen soon, so it might as well be now, so he doesn't have to be sick anymore, right? My dad has had cancer since I was in kindergarten, for as long as I can really remember. It hasn't always been visible, but during every memory I have of my dad, he was sick with cancer. My mom told me that probably within the next month, he won't be sick anymore. So it's okay that I've been praying that, right? It isn't bad of me?"

I stopped talking, and I put down my hands in my lap to give my fingers a break. Slowly, I lifted my head up to look at my friends sitting around me. Each of them were staring back at me, their cheeks red and wet with tears, their eyes swollen, and their noses sniffling. I hadn't realized how much what I was saying was affecting them until I looked at their faces.

This whole situation my family was going through was horrible. But it didn't seem real. It seemed like we were watching a sad movie that we were really invested in, but it could be turned off by the click of a remote, and life would automatically switch back to normal, and everything would be okay again. Looking into the faces of my best friends, I saw that it wasn't going to happen. This problem wasn't going to go away with a simple push of a button. My dad was dying. Sometime very soon, my dad was going to die.

CHAPTER 12

"TIME TO GET UP!" MOM was practically singing it throughout the house. 2:15 in the morning is too early for anything anyway, but there should be a rule written against singing this early. I knew Mom was a morning person, but until this morning, I thought even she had her limits.

I crawled out to the living room to find Claire sitting straight up like a zombie, hair standing up in every direction, and drool crusted on the side of her open mouth. Emma was passed out next to her. What a sight.

The train was scheduled to leave at 3:30 a.m., and after an hour delay, we took off to head west. One of my dad's many uncles offered us his beach house in Oregon, along with his pickup truck, for an entire week. It was already August, so we had school to start thinking about, but we needed to get away, just the four of us. Dad's absence was hanging so heavily at home that in order to learn how be a family without him, we needed to simply be somewhere else for a little while.

It had been years since we had been able to go on a vacation without either bringing Dad and making sure he was okay or leaving him at home and having to call to check up on him every so often. It was just the four of us girls now, and we didn't have a choice but to learn how to live with that.

I stared out the window of the train that was taking us west, as far west as we could go. I had seen hundreds of trains in my life, but I had never traveled on one. I didn't know that they rocked back and forth on the tracks so much that it felt like we could derail at any second. And we had thirty-three hours of this.

Mom had asked the three of us if we wanted to go to the viewing car to play cards, but I didn't want to play cards. That was always Mom's response to any kind of free time. Sitting with the family at home? Let's play cards. Just had dinner? Let's play cards. Dad dies so we have more people over than we ever have had to host before? Let's play cards. I didn't want to play anymore. Emma and Claire were riding Mom's card train, but not me. I just wanted to sit there, CD player in my lap, headphones strapped over my ears, and stare out at the fields of grass that sped by and went on forever.

JULY 20, 2006

Tom died last night with the same grace and dignity with which he lived his life. Over the past week, I saw him lose different pleasures every day. He lost interest in eating, watching TV, getting out of bed, and eventually drinking. The nurses would come in to take care of him, and I know that they knew more than they were telling me. As with all new things, I was curious about what they were doing and what I should be doing. We switched from oral medications to topical gels. We switched from drinks of water to little blue sponges on a stick. I asked many questions and told the nurses of my observations, and they always had solutions to keep Tom comfortable.

Every time the nurses visited, they asked if Tom was in pain. They kept offering more pain medication, but he never seemed to be uncomfortable or in pain. This seemed to surprise the nurses. Of all the vital statistics that the nurses looked at, I chose to pay attention to Tom's blood pressure. These numbers are rounded, but you can see the steady decline. His normal pressure was 140/90. It dropped to 118/82 which is considered to be fantastic for most people, but to me it signaled a drastic change. It kept dropping; 80/60, 60/40, and yesterday it was 48/32.

When his blood pressure got that low, along with several other indicators, I knew it was time to call his family. Tom had many visitors, and I'm certain that he knew who they all were. Even on his last day when he didn't respond to anything, I got right into his face and told him I was there. He responded the best that he could with a low grunt. That was enough for me so I knew that he knew I was there.

Having never dealt with death before, I was concerned and curious about the final moments. But Tom's moments were as peaceful as you could pray and hope for. My sister was in the room with him, and she heard him take a breath that sounded different than normal. She was about to get me when Lisa and I walked in the room. I looked at Beth and then went and touched Tom's chest. He took one breath, and as I walked around the bed to the other side, he took his final breath. He went peacefully and without pain, surrounded by three people who were special to him.

I was able to touch his right leg without causing him pain for the first time in years. We prayed around his bedside, we cried many tears for our loss, and we were grateful that his suffering had ended. His parents and brothers arrived in the evening and were able to spend some precious moments with him.

Tom is out of pain, and he is jogging, playing softball, enjoying the outdoors, camping, working on computers, and doing all the things he loved about living.

Thank you for loving Tom. He loved all of you.

God is amazing, the girls are amazing, and Tom's life was amazing. I will continue on this amazing journey, deeply saddened by my loss, but eternally grateful to have experienced Tom DeJong and everything that he was. The girls and I will not let Tom be forgotten — we will live our lives in honor of him.

We love you all, in God's name,
TBEMC

CHAPTER 13

THE BEACH HOUSE WAS SIMPLE. It had a living room, kitchen, bathroom, and stairs that led up to two bedrooms and another bathroom. It was perfect. We got there at night, so we weren't really able to make out our surroundings. We decided it would be best to get some sleep and go explore in the morning with some daylight.

When I woke up in the morning, it took me a few seconds to remember where I was and what we were doing there. I slipped out of the bed that I was sharing with Claire and made my way down the stairs to find Mom sitting and doing a crossword puzzle in the living room. I walked up to a window to see what the area looked like by daylight. All I could see from where I stood were trees, other small houses, and that it had rained overnight. There was standing water everywhere. I turned to head toward where Mom was sitting.

"Morning," I said.

"Good morning," she said as she looked up from her puzzle with a smile on her face. "Are your sisters still sleeping?" I nodded and went to sit down on the couch near her.

She scribbled a note in the corner of her page, closed the book, set it on the end table next to her chair, looked at me, and said, "Let's go explore."

"What? Shouldn't we wait for Emma and Claire?"

"Oh, we'll only do a little exploring," she said as she got up from the chair. "Just enough to find a cool coffee shop or something."

"Okay." I smiled at her. "Let me find a sweatshirt."

I grabbed something warmer to throw on over what I was already wearing and headed outside to meet up with Mom. She always talked about how she loved doing things with the whole family, but she also liked being able to spend some time alone with each of us. I loved when that was with me.

I was about to grab the doorknob to head outside when I heard a massive thud on the other side of the door. I whipped the door open to find Mom sprawled across the stairs, lying still, but breathing heavily.

"Mom? Are you okay? What happened?"

"I don't know. I slipped on the wet stairs and fell on my tailbone. I'm waiting to see what hurts." It took her a minute, but she slowly got herself to her feet, and after poking herself in search of pain, we decided that she was just going to have a nice bruise, and we could still go exploring for a cappuccino.

CHAPTER 14

WE ALL AGREED THAT OREGON was so beautiful that we needed to spend a little bit of every day sightseeing. We went on drives through the hills that looked out onto the beaches and shores, we walked through small towns filled with local shops and fish-and-chips stands, and we tried as many restaurants as we could.

After driving on winding streets parallel with the ocean, we decided to stop and get out to enjoy the beach. We knew the water was only about fifty degrees, but the views were worth it. Even if the water was a frigid temperature, we had to at least touch it. We couldn't do this at home.

There was a sort of pier of rocks and boulders of all different sizes that extended out into the ocean. I made sure I was in front so I could lead the way. "Come this way," I told them. "If you take this path, we can get pretty far out into the water without getting wet." Emma climbed behind me, Claire was behind her, and Mom followed in the back. This brought me back to elementary school gym classes when we'd play Mission Impossible. But this time, instead of avoiding touching the gym floor, we were trying to avoid touching the bitterly cold ocean water.

I stopped and leaned backwards toward Emma, my arm outstretched to offer her some help getting from rock to rock. She accepted, but pulled me by the hand as if I was glued to the ground.

"Careful," I yelled at her. "Don't pull me in."

"Then don't put out your arm," she snapped back.

"Jeez," Claire said.

"You girls go ahead," Mom called at us from behind, a little winded. "I'll catch up." Claire started giggling, amused by Mom's slower pace and clear inability to climb and balance on the wet rocks. I climbed past Emma and Claire to go back to where Mom was studying the rocks and a possible path in front of her.

"Here, let me help you." I found a path to get her from where she stood to where we were, avoiding the most obstacles. I pointed the way as I explained what to do.

"That's fine," she said. Before I could respond, she bent at both of her knees and stepped straight into the ice cold water which swallowed up the entire lower half of her legs, all the way up to her knees. She gasped, stood completely still, and squeezed her eyes shut.

"What in the world?" I asked her. "Are you nuts? It's freezing in there. Can you even feel your feet?"

"Yes, I know that," she said slowly. "I was likely going to fall in anyway. Now I just got into the water on my own terms." I turned around to see Claire staring, her eyes wide and mouth hanging open, and Emma hunched over laughing, tears streaming down her face.

On our last night in Oregon before we had to go back to North Dakota, back to reality, we all agreed there was no better way to take advantage of this beautiful place than to spend our time on the beach. Once we arrived, we all separated to enjoy the scenery in our own ways. Mom stayed away from the water and was searching for a small piece of driftwood to take home as a souvenir. Emma had found a small hut on the sand, put together with logs, and she went to go explore it, and Claire walked up to the edge of the shore to put her toes in the water. I walked in the other direction.

The sand was cold and hard underneath my shoes, and the air was muggy, heavy with the smell of fish. It was weird to think about getting back home and going back to school. School is such a normal idea, and our lives had just become anything but normal. Playing basketball, struggling through math class, going to church on Sundays, taking family vacations, watching Duke during the March Madness tournament — how was I going to do any of these without Dad?

I looked down the length of the beach at my sisters, and I wondered what they were thinking. What were they going to miss? The things I would miss the most about my dad were personal stories and jokes that he and I shared. I would miss his laugh, and I would miss his facial expressions, and the way he joked and always laughed at his own jokes. I would miss the way he smelled and how he loved each of us in such different ways. I breathed in deeply through my nose to fill my lungs with the salty air. I looked up at the sky as I slowly let the air back out again. The sky was streaked in pink, and there were seagulls flying overhead. It was like a scene out of a movie. We were about to leave and head back to something resembling normalcy. It was painful to think about, but I had a feeling I was getting myself ready to face it.

Mom was calling me over to where the three of them were now standing together, and as I got closer to them, I saw that she was holding a small plastic cup in her hands. It looked like Tupperware with a lid snapped onto the top, and I had a feeling, before she even spoke, that I knew what she was going to say.

"Let's spread his ashes all over the place," she said. "I want to put some in front of his gravesite in South Dakota by the rest of his family. I want to put him in his favorite places in the mountains in Colorado and on his favorite golf courses. He would have wanted to come to his uncle's beach house with his girls, so I think it's only fitting that we put him in the ocean, too."

We didn't say anything, but we all nodded our heads a little in agreement. Mom took a step into the water, and without reacting to the temperature, she removed the cup's lid and poured a small amount of what looked like sand into the ocean. I watched the ashes land on the water. Some floated, and some slowly drifted down the few inches of water to mix in with the sand. As a wave crashed toward our feet, the tide pulled all of the ashes out into the ocean.

Mom turned around and handed the cup to Emma, who stepped forward and poured out her own little bit of Dad's ashes. Then it was my turn.

I stepped into the water with my mom and sisters standing behind me, and I felt the sting of the cold water on my ankles. I looked into the cup that I was holding in my hand. It was pale sand with a few larger pieces mixed in. I wondered where these ashes would go. The water would take it away, but where would it go? What places would Dad end up that he had never been before?

There was a small burning sensation building up behind my eyes. I blinked hard to fight back any tears that were trying to form, and I looked into the cup at the ashes again. Without another thought, I tipped it on its side and let some fall into the water at my feet. My heart broke.

The moment the ashes hit the water I wanted them back. I wanted to put his ashes back into the cup and snap on the lid so they were safe. I had to let so much of my dad go that I just wanted to hold onto any last piece of him that I had left.

On the short drive back to the beach house, I sat in the back seat of the pickup and leaned into the window. I let the tears stream down my cheeks, but I didn't let myself cry hard enough to make any sound, or change the level of my breathing. In the morning, we would go home. I didn't know who I would go to when I was overwhelmed. I didn't know who would be there with me to sneak our own snacks into basketball games. I didn't know who would keep my mom company when my sisters and I all left for college and our adult lives. I didn't know who was going to walk me down the aisle at my wedding. I didn't know who my future children would call "Grandpa."

What I did know was that I had a wonderful mom and amazing sisters. And we had an incredible support system of family and as-good-as-family friends, who would always be there for us whenever we felt the hole in our lives that would never be filled. We lost a man that we would never be able to, or want to, replace.

JULY 20, 2007

One year — the nineteenth came with some relief and some regret. The past year was much easier than I ever expected. I'm not saying that there weren't tears and sad times, but mostly when I thought of Tom, I smiled and was grateful that he had been a wonderful part of my life. I think I never realized, or allowed myself to realize, how much stress was involved with dealing with cancer and all that goes with it for seven years. This past year has been very relaxing emotionally. Whenever I hear of someone facing their battle with cancer, or an equally horrible illness, I feel sorrow, but deep down a sense of relief that it isn't us anymore.

I also regret that the first year is over. I, of course, have spent many times remembering "what we were doing a year ago." I don't want the memories and

feelings of Tom to fade. I want him to stay in our
thoughts every day. I don't like the thought that he
has been gone for over a year. Is it good or bad that
I can still see him walk through the door, hear him
talk, and smell him? I'm going with good.

Yesterday, I had coffee with my best friend. I
had phone calls, cards, and flowers from friends and
family. The girls and I visited Tom's office and had
lunch at one of his favorite fast food restaurants. We
watched Mary's basketball game and ended the evening
eating hotdogs and ice cream sundaes with friends.
Thank you to everyone.

My girls are amazing. One thing I miss most is
sharing their smallest accomplishments with their
father. No one else but a parent truly appreciates how
they fell down and didn't cry, their large burp at the
dinner table (dads only), the sparkle in their eyes
when they talk about their passions. So, if you'll
bear with me, I must brag for a moment.

Emma - she is in Indiana right now for a Presbyterian
Youth Triennium. She will be gone until Tuesday. I
will be anxious to hear every detail, but I know that
I will only get a brief outline of what happened.
She is so mature, and I am learning that she will
lead her own life apart from me. I do treasure our
spontaneous late-night discussions. She got all As for
her sophomore year, she loves volleyball, and she took
summer school PE so that she will have more time for
more classes next year. She made the madrigals singing
group, which meets before school. She is going to try
out for volleyball, which would meet after school.
Emma finds delight and enjoyment in things that are

slightly odd and different. Her perspectives on life are always cheerful and positive. She makes me smile, and I thank God for her every day.

Mary - my athlete and social butterfly. Basketball will always be her passion. She is truly alive when she is on the court. While I strive to understand the game a little more every season, I couldn't be more in step with her every move on the court. She has managed to injure herself twice this past year, both times resulting in x-rays and crutches. She tore some ligaments last week but found it most painful to sit on the bench and watch her teammates play when she couldn't. Her goal is to be back on the court by tournament time next Tuesday. Mary has a large group of friends, and the drama that goes on in the middle school is never dull. She loves to be online talking with about forty people at one time. She got all As for her eighth grade year. She can get her driving permit whenever she gets around to studying for the test. Mary likes to venture out with friends but is always most comfortable at home at the end of the day. I love having her close by, and I thank God for her every day.

Claire - how can my baby be going to middle school? I'm not really happy about this fact. I know she is ready, but am I? Claire doesn't have a passion for any one thing. She has a passion for everything. I suppose anything that has to do with the fine arts really captures her attention. She is in theater this summer, she dances at church, and she is trying out her skills with volleyball. She has one more year where she can do a little bit of everything, and then she will have to start making some choices because the seasons will overlap. Claire got all As in fifth grade. She is looking forward to soccer, dance, Awana, and all of her activities starting up again in the fall. Claire's energy keeps me young, and I thank God for her every day.

I have been busy with the girls, church, and friends. I have been thinking about returning to the workforce, and when the right job comes along, I will know it. My main focus right now is keeping us all happy and healthy. For the most part, we are happy, and if I can keep Mary off of crutches, then we have been healthy.

Each of us has helped make our new family work. Through all that we have been through, and all that we have yet to experience, we know that God is our guide. We follow Him with complete confidence and love.

In God's name,
BEMC

AFTERWORD

CLAIRE

Because I was only ten years old when I lost my dad, it's hard to say if it was harder or easier because I was so young. I was three when he first got cancer, and because of that, I don't have memories of my dad when he was healthy. Frankly, I have hardly any memories of my dad at all: my dad and me having pizza nights while my mom and sisters were at youth group, our nightly routine of him reciting the many nicknames he had for me, and riding home from church and my dad letting go of the wheel so that I would be forced to steer the Jeep. The rest of my memories are only because of stories and pictures.

I am never sad that I am not able to have clear memories because I know every day how much he loved me and cared for me. My mom will tell me how much I am like him. We both are very easygoing and carefree. Neither of us fights or gets into arguments with people. We both have a love for mathematics. He was a math teacher who became a statistician. For me, I have taken that love towards my engineering career. While I can see my mom's eyes glaze over when I talk about gear ratios and structural stability, I know that he would be able to talk to me about calculus and statistics.

It will always be hard to have lost my dad so young. I think about how I was never able to be a stereotypical teenage girl who rolls her eyes at her dad, I won't be able to have my dad walk me down the wedding aisle, and my kids will never know their biological grandfather. But I am able to appreciate how truly lucky and blessed I am. I have a family who only grew stronger through tragedy. My mother is engaged, and I have gained a second family through this wonderful man. I have been in a relationship with my boyfriend for over two years, who bravely battled cancer as well. Our mutual understanding of this disease has allowed us to grow closer in a more loving relationship.

In this book, I was able to not only remember my father, but to learn more about him. At times, it was tough to read, and I had to take breaks to compose myself. But I'm glad that others will have the chance to learn about the wonderful man I am lucky to call my dad.

MARY

I haven't seen my dad since I was thirteen. I haven't seen my dad walk normally, in the way that he walks without a cane or crutches, or even limping, since I was ten. I was worried that I wouldn't be able to remember these small details about him so many years later, but I found that when I started to write about my memories of him, it all came back. As I typed, my mind went all the way back into the places I had been. I could see the people who were there. I remembered things exactly as they were.

I think of my dad often; there are so many things that remind me of him, but it seems that with time, he has become more of a memory of a memory, if that makes sense. I remember small pieces at a time, maybe the way his laugh sounds or a still image of what he looks like or the smell of his cologne. But not often do more than one of these pieces come to me at once. Writing the details of these memories brought all of it back, all of it at once. It isn't something that makes me sad, as someone may think. Instead, it's made him a full and complete memory again, and it's been refreshing to see and spend time with him.

It's funny — until I revisited all of these times, I had forgotten how basketball was the most important thing in my life. It was my entertainment, my stress-reliever, my focus, and my drive. I lived and breathed basketball, and my dad did it with me. After we lost him, I continued with basketball. I remember a time when I was in eighth grade in one of our traveling tournaments, we played with only five players (due to injuries) against the toughest team. After losing the game by only one point, I had told my mom that I wished I could tell Dad about the game. I wanted to remember it so I could tell him about it when I got to heaven someday. She told me that, hopefully, I will live a long time and have more important things to tell him about than my middle school basketball games.

I continued playing basketball through high school, and after I graduated college with an English education degree, I accepted a job in Minot, North Dakota teaching English and coaching girls' basketball. I spent my three years working in Minot as a sophomore girls' basketball coach and an assistant coach to the junior varsity and varsity teams. It astounded me how much I still hadn't known about the game until I began coaching.

While in Minot, I met the man I will marry, Michael, and together in the summer of 2018, we moved to Denver, Colorado to follow his job promotion as a chemist in an oil company, and this is where we live now.

My mom lost her husband of almost twenty years, leaving her alone to continue raising three teenage girls. We were blessed with grandparents, aunts and uncles, family friends, and a church family, but still, in our day-to-day lives, it was just the four of us. My mom has since told me that she had to be both the father and mother in her parenting decisions. She had to play both good cop and bad cop with any boyfriends, and she had to give us advice and guidance without a partner to discuss each unique situation. She will attend our weddings and watch as our grandpa, in place of his son, walks us each down the aisle, and she has done all of this through her faith in God. Her strength is something that I will never forget and will always respect.

Shortly after Dad passed away, after he was cremated, my mom approached the three of us with a unique idea. She told us that she would like to order us necklaces that were urns, so we could carry him with us wherever we went throughout our lives. We had a choice between silver and gold, and a choice between a heart, a teardrop, or a cross. She made us choose privately so we did not influence each other's decisions. I have worn my necklace every day since I was thirteen years old. My sisters and I all have our necklaces, our identical silver teardrop necklaces.

EMMA

One of my clearest memories from the morning of the funeral is that I didn't have enough time to get my hair done. I was fifteen when my dad died, and I was very much a fifteen-year-old girl in how I experienced it (that is to say, with a thick lens of self-focus). I was sad, but I had no idea how to handle the emotion.

One of the things that makes me saddest now, twelve years later, is that I never got to know my dad as an adult. Since he died, I've become a Christian, married my husband, and had a bunch of kids. There is so much I want to share with him, and even more, so much I want to know about him.

And then came this book. Mary, I'm so grateful you've written this. The emails showed me some of his writing that I'd never read before. Your flashbacks gave me a perspective I never had. The visitation gave me a description of Dad that was growing vague. I still long to talk with him, but having these memories captured in a book is truly a treasure.

Luke, my husband, also loved reading this because it gave him a way to get to know Dad outside of my stories and my perspective. Luke and I have been married for five years, and the Lord has blessed us with Asher (three), Lewis (two), and Nora (ten months). We live in Brookings, South Dakota, and Luke does full-time college ministry. I get to help him in that, alongside my role as chief of domestic operations (*aka* stay-at-home mom).

I'm grateful I was raised by a dad who truly loved my sisters and me, and having kids of my own gives me an even deeper appreciation of this. I'm sad he was taken when he was, but I never doubt his unconditional love. I have clear memories of him *truly enjoying* me, and I'll be thankful if my kids can someday say the same.

BECKY

I never wanted to set foot in Roger Maris Cancer Center again. After spending seven years there with Tom, I thought it was a thing of the past. It is funny how God has his own plans. I stayed home with the girls and spent time re-organizing our life at home. I got more closet space and figured out what all the tools in the garage were used for. As the girls became more independent, it was time for me to venture out of the house. I worked for three years at a nursing home in the coffee shop and then, against all advice and reason, I took a greeter position at the cancer center. I have been working there for almost eight years. Every day is humbling and rewarding. I get to hear patients' stories, give hugs, show pictures of my children and grandchildren, and share Tom's story when it seems appropriate.

I have been blessed with Bob. He is a kind, caring man who loves my family and me. We met shortly after I began working at the cancer center. He, too, lost his spouse to cancer. This common bond has allowed us to continue to love Tom and Mona, and to move forward in life. Together, we are busy with five daughters and their families, we love to travel, and we value our quiet moments together when we realize that we are fortunate to have found each other.

I have allowed many memories of our cancer journey to fade. Reading this book has brought them all back. What I realize is that the pain and hard times have faded a lot, and the happy memories have stayed with me. My girls remind me of their dad; sharing stories with Bob and at work remind me of Tom; and in quiet, unexpected moments I remember our special, private times. I met Tom when I was a senior in high school, I got married when I was twenty-two, and we were married for almost twenty years. Tom will always be in my heart.

Emma, Mary, and Tom

Family

Family in Colorado

Mary and Claire

Mary in driveway decorated by friends

Young Tom and Becky

Tom and Mary

Tom and Mary

Tom and Mary at Relay for Life

Tom and Mary camping

Tom and Mary playing basketball

Young Tom

Young Tom

CPSIA information can be obtained
at www.ICGtesting.com
Printed in the USA
LVHW092138281019
635642LV00008B/105/P

9 781633 939066